PASTORAL RELATEDNESS

---

the essence of pastoral care

John Quinlan

University Press of America,® Inc.
Lanham · New York · Oxford

University Press of America,® Inc.
4720 Boston Way
Lanham, Maryland 20706
UPA Acquisitions Department (301) 459-3366

12 Hid's Copse Rd.
Cumnor Hill, Oxford OX2 9JJ

Printed in the United States of America
British Library Cataloging in Publication Information Available

ISBN 0-7618-2262-3 (pbk. : alk. paper)

™ The paper used in this publication meets the minimum requirements of American National Standard for Information Sciences—Permanence of Paper for Printed Library Materials, ANSI Z39.48—1984

Dedicated to my late parents Paddy and Nancy Quinlan,
who worked as a general practitioner and a nurse,
and whose caring included and extended beyond
the medical model.

Contents

List of Figures

List of Tables

Permissions

Michael Kearney, Consultant in Palliative Medicine, Our Lady's Hospice and St. Vincent's Hospital, Dublin, Ireland, for permission to reprint his illustration of 'The Surface Mind and Deep Mind (Psychological Model).'

Preface

My immediate family background is rooted in healthcare. Both my parents, my father as a doctor in general practice and my mother as a nurse, worked together from our home in Kenmare, Co. Kerry, a rural town in southwest Ireland. My closeness to this work and lifestyle from my earliest days influenced me deeply. My parents' commitment, dedication and caring inspired me. I felt drawn to a caring profession either in medicine or in priesthood. I opted for the priesthood and was appointed to serve as a hospital chaplain.

In the context in which I began hospital chaplaincy, the expectations were low. In the hospital context of the time and in the almost exclusively Roman Catholic tradition, the chaplain was merely expected, on request, to celebrate sacraments with critically ill people. He (it was all men at that time) was a peripheral member of the caring team, far from being an integral part of it. Part-time chaplains were the norm. I did not accept this and from the beginning of my ministry, though a part-time chaplain, spent almost all of my working hours in the hospital.

I loved this work and spent several hours daily working in the hospital, developing a fuller chaplaincy service, ensuring that I initiated pastoral visits with patients and took referrals from staff. I tried to be attentive to ministry to patients' relatives and to staff persons, and to teamwork with staff of all disciplines.

Granger Westberg noted that working in the hospital setting

caused a crisis of vocation for some clinical pastoral care-givers, as they were in awe of the healing power of modern medicine and wondered about the paucity of their contribution.[1] I did not experience a crisis of vocation, but I did wonder about my contribution and the contribution of pastoral care to holistic healthcare and healing. Patients, relatives, and staff expressed satisfaction with pastoral care. This feedback was unsolicited. I was puzzled. Why were they satisfied? With what aspects of pastoral care were they satisfied? Were some aspects of pastoral care more helpful than others? If so, how is this effected?

Thus began the search and research, which I hoped would go some way towards answering these questions. It has clarified much for me. I hope it will be of assistance to others with similar questions, and to anyone interested in the discipline of pastoral care.

[1]William M. Sullivan, "A New Ecology of Healing: Medicine and Religion in Holistic Care," *Listening* 19 (September 1984): 109.

Acknowledgements

This work is based on my Doctor of Ministry thesis, which was completed with the invaluable assistance of some of the staff of the School of Theology at Boston University. In this regard I thank Carrie Doehring Ph.D., Assistant Professor of Pastoral Psychology Nancy Gieseler Devor Ph.D., Adjunct Professor of Pastoral Psychology, Raymond Van de Moortell Ph.D., Lecturer in Theology, Chris Schlauch Ph.D., Assistant Professor of Pastoral Psychology and Psychology of Religion, and Wesley Wildman Ph.D., Associate Professor of Theology and Ethics. Gearoid O'Donoghue Ph.D. of the Institute of Technology, Tralee, Co. Kerry, Ireland willingly gave of his time and expertise in statistics. My colleagues on the Pastoral Care team in Tralee General Hospital, Edward Barrett, Michael O'Doherty, and Eileen Mullins generously took more than their share of the workload while this work was researched. I thank my co-researchers, Joan Cotter, Joan Gaynor, Juliana Murphy, Mairead Murphy, and Martin O'Sullivan. I thank Ann Hanley, Director of the Council for Research and Development, Maynooth, Ireland for permission to reprint figures from the July 1997 unpublished "Religious Confidence Study." Thanks to Pat O'Driscoll, Information Technology Manager at Tralee General Hospital, for his help and patience with the computer. I thank Diana Lavery, UPA Acquisitions, Beverly Baum, Production Editor, and Cynthia Archie, Marketing Manager at University Press of America for their professionalism and support. Thanks to Thomas King for his patient typesetting. There are many others who contributed greatly, management staff, other pastoral care colleagues, nursing, clerical, and medical staff at the hospital. The many parts were a single unit. Thank you all very much.

Introduction

I formulated the thesis that pastoral relatedness is the essence of pastoral care. Pastoral relatedness is that special quality of the pastoral relationship that helps a person access his/her deeper spiritual self, thus enabling the person to experience God's care in his/her suffering. It facilitates enough closeness to allow a person disclose what is intimate or innermost in the person's life, yet is distant enough to allow the intimate zone to be vacated when this is required.[1] It embraces love, trust, respect, warmth, active listening, understanding, compassion, honesty, graciousness, genuineness, sensitivity, judgment free attitude, equality, fidelity, acceptance, and hope, all contained in a caring 'being-with.' I am sure I have not exhausted this list. Pastoral Relatedness is a holistic concept; the whole of the experience in greater than the sum of the individual aspects. Various pastoral relationships will possess varying degrees of pastoral relatedness.

A crucial variant is the capacity of the pastor to enter into pastoral relationships of this nature.

Pastoral care is 'being with' the other as one who cares. Care is attitude and action that seeks the best interest of the other. It is being positively disposed towards the other, and this attitude is expressed in concrete acts. The word 'care' is derived from the Gothic word 'kara,' meaning 'to lament with,' 'to journey with,' to 'be with.'[2] Care is pastoral when its focus is beyond the human. It is "a helping encounter in the dimension of ultimate concern. Its function is to communicate the power of the Divine, which is eternal, and which conquers all forces of non-being. It is the power, which mediates the courage to accept finitude and the anxiety of creatureliness.[3] "Care becomes uniquely pastoral when it helps to direct others to the source of life and power, to that which alone is infinite and eternal."[4] Pastoral care facilitates the search for meaning in life and in death.

Part I, The Meaning of Pastoral Care, in seeking to demonstrate the thesis theoretically, embraces both theology and psychology. I searched in theology for the deeper meaning and for an answer to the question 'why pastoral care?' and in psychology for an answer to 'how does good pastoral care affect the person?' Part II tests the theory by scientifically researching it. This research was both quantitative and qualitative in the use of a questionnaire and interviews with patients. The findings demonstrate that there is a high level of satisfaction with each aspect of pastoral care namely, Acceptance of the Chaplain's Ministry, the Chaplain's Supportive Ministry, the Chaplain's Ministry to Help the Patient Cope, and the Chaplain's Ministry to the Patient's Private Concerns, the highest correlation being between Patient Satisfaction and Ministry to the Patient's Private Concerns.

The person and skills of the pastor, which enable pastoral relatedness, help a person to share his/her private concerns and have them heard. This helps the person cope with his/her situation, and facilitates supportive ministry. Outcome research demonstrates that pastoral care contributes to patients' 'getting better faster,' to their 'readiness to go home,' and to 'making hospitalization easier.'

1. Indebted to M. C. Madden, "Intimacy and Distance," in *Dictionary of Pastoral Care and Counseling*, ed. Rodney J. Hunter (Nashville: Abingdon Press, 1990), 799.
2. Henri J.M. Nouwen, *Out of Solitude* (Notre Dame, IN: Ave Maria Press, 1974), 34.
3. Paul Tillich, "The Theology of Pastoral Care," *Pastoral Psychology*, 10 no. 97 (1959): 22.
4. Lawrence E. Holst, ed., *Hospital Ministry: The Role of the Chaplain Today* (New York: Crossroad, 1985), 46.

Part I

The Meaning of Pastoral Care

Chapter 1

The Heart of Pastoral Care

Christian pastoral care is based on the message of Jesus, which is love. Over the centuries from the time of Jesus and the early Chuch, through the following centuries, and to the current emphases of the twentieth century pastoral care movement, the thinking and administration of pastoral care has changed.

Traditions and Theology of Care in the Old Testament

From its foundation, the Judeo-Christian tradition has understood relationship to be the heart of pastoral care. "While there is no single theology of pastoral care in the Old Testament and the Apocrypha there is evidence of considerable concern with the subject. In general, the goal of care according to the Old Testament is the maintenance and restoration of relationships among human beings, between human beings and God, and of human beings with the world."[1]

The leading theme of the Old Testament is God's care for God's people. The care of people for one another is derived from God's divine care. The goal of care is to maintain or restore relationships between God and people, and among people. Biblical care is communal. The health and peace of individual persons is both affected by and affects the community. In ancient Israel there were specialized roles directly concerned with the care of individuals. There were structures in place whereby someone would 'be with' a person in trouble. This was seen as evidence of God's intervention in human affairs, in terms of God's covenant of love and care for God's people. The Psalter demonstrates the caring theme - persons suffering illness or crisis prayed for care from God. They expressed anger, frustration, and gratitude about care received.

The Pastoral Care of Jesus and Pastoral Care in the New Testament

Between them, A. J. Malherbe,[2] Blaine B. Radar,[3] and J. I. H. McDonald[4] have considered the pastoral care of Jesus and pastoral care in the New Testament. Malherbe and Radar note the fact that, when the New Testament was written, the traditions about Jesus had been adapted to the needs of the early Church. The Gospels and the rest of the New Testament reflect the church's conceptions of Jesus rather than those of Jesus himself. Radar, in his research, acknowledges that it is impossible to describe Jesus' ministry apart from the impression Jesus made on his followers and on the early Church. Nevertheless, he attempted to focus on the concrete ministry of Jesus by considering the role of Jesus as minister, and the central motifs underlying Jesus' concrete pastoral care to people in distress. Malberbe and McDonald consider the pastoral care of Jesus as interpreted by the early Church and as presented in the New Testament.

The central motifs of Jesus' concrete pastoral care with people can be conceptualized as servant, shepherd, sonship, and healing. In relation to service, Radar refers to Matthew 2:28 (JB) "the Son of Man came not to be served but to serve" (See also Lk. 22:27 and Jn. 13:4-11). Jesus' entire ministry was based on service of God and of others. Shepherding involves leading, nurturing, guiding, guarding, sharing, sacrificing and much more (Jn. 21:15-27). Care and love of, and from, the Father characterized sonship (Jn. 15:15-27). This attitude is to be shown in action towards others. Healing reflects the action of Jesus the healer. There are several passages referring to Jesus as healer for example, "No doubt you will quote me the saying, 'Physician, heal yourself.'" (Lk. 4:23 JB). Jesus healing works were expressions of his own compassion, supernatural signs of Jesus' proclamation of God's kingdom, and of God working through God's chosen person.

J. I. H. McDonald notes the prominence of the image of shepherd in both the Old Testament and the Gospels. The shepherd "seeks the lost, brings back the strayed, binds up the crippled, strengthens the weak, watches over the strong, and will feed them in justice" (Ezek. 34:16 RSV). McDonald links this to Jesus' sonship. The bond of trust between the shepherd and his flock reflects the bond of trust between the Father and Son. The shepherd knows his flock personally, nourishes them, and cares for them (See Jn. 10:7-18). The healing is in the relationship.

Jesus' followers experienced the benefit of his pastoral care. He was their model for pastoral care and they sought to extend care to others. The nature and essence of Jesus' pastoral care, through shepherding and healing, is a trusting relationship, based on the relationship between the Father and Son.

The Early Church

As the early Church developed, structures for the administration of pastoral care emerged. Those sent by Jesus were to continue his mission of preaching, healing and serving. Jesus appointed and commissioned the Twelve to carry the gospel to the world, to baptize, to forgive sins, and to heal (Mk. 3:13-19; Mt. 28:18-20). This command was taken to imply authority to govern. The Twelve appointed seven for the pastoral care of the Hellenistic widows (Acts 6:1-6). These seven were ordained with prayer and the laying on of hands.

Other leadership roles emerged for the provision and co-ordination of the pastoral care of people. These roles were those of bishops, elders, and deacons. The bishop was the chief pastor of the flock. The elders served him as advisors and deputized for him in his absence. The deacons were his assistants in worship and pastoral visitation. Other ministries of pastoral care, which were exercised by the faithful, emerged. These included giving aid, healing, helping, teaching, and evangelizing. One of these other ministries was that of pastor. The pastor was the person who attended to the daily needs of the flock. It is clear from Paul's letter to the Romans that women and men were engaged in these ministries. Paul records the work of Phoebe, Mary, Tryphaena and Tryphosa (Romans 16:1; 16:6; 16:12).

A Change of Emphasis in Pastoral Care

L. O. Mills,[5] W. H. C. Frend,[6] J. D. Creighton,[7] and Blaine B. Radar[8] outline the history of pastoral care.

As the first century came to a close and Christians were more and more becoming a separate community, new emphases in pastoral care began to emerge. The earlier Christians had expected an imminent return of Christ and paid much attention to grace and forgiveness in preparation for the Second Coming of Christ. Frend writes that down to the middle of the second century pastoral care, whether under the supervision of the bishop or not, was considered among the duties of every Christian towards another person.[9]

As Christians began to realize that Christ's Second Coming might not be as imminent as they first assumed, pastoral care gradually became the special function of the bishop and of the clergy. The Church became concerned with those Christians who compromised and lapsed. This signaled a shift from the positive emphasis on grace and forgiveness to a demand for moral conduct. This emphasis, in one form or another, was to dominate pastoral care for seventeen centuries. Practices and attitudes that started as the mutual pastoral concern of Christians for one another became an elaborate penitential system supervised by the bishop and his representatives. Repentance became associated with penance for sins. However, at all times throughout the centuries, exhortation to perform caring acts always remained.

An example of this was the work of Vincent de Paul (1580-1660) and his followers. Through his founding of the Sisters of Charity, Vincent de Paul brought nuns out of the cloisters and they worked among the poor. This began in the Paris slums. These were the first nursing sisters. They visited sick people and helped keep them clean and fed and as comfortable as possible. Many hospitals, where doctors practiced modern medicine and nursing nuns nursed, were founded. Arguably the most noteworthy is the Mayo Clinic in Rochester, Minnesota, which was opened on November 1st 1887 by the Mayo brothers, doctors, helped by nursing nuns. It should be noted that the motivation of nursing nuns was primarily spiritual. Their works of mercy helped towards their own salvation and dispensed supernatural grace to their patients. They used their nursing skills as a way of having their spiritual message heard.

During the Middle Ages preoccupation with the necessity of sacraments led to abuses, not least of which was the sale of indulgences. Indulgences had emerged as a way of remitting all or some of the penance needed to restore the person to reconciliation with God. Some people believed that the purchase of indulgences assured salvation. These abuses led to the Protestant Reformation, which sought to correct the abuses. Protestant pastoral care centered on preaching and on communion.

Carter Lindberg, borrowing from John T. McNeill, states that most scholars agree that pastoral care and counseling of the sick took root in the Reformation.[10] It is easy to see how this follows from Luther's philosophy and theology. The doctrine of justification by faith alone, apart from works, allowed people to channel their energy into secular vocations as a way of expressing their spiritual call.

Roman Catholic pastoral care continued to revolve around the sacramental system. The Council of Trent, 1552-63, was the Roman Catholic Church's response to the Protestant Reformation. It corrected many of the abuses that had developed around penitential discipline. It redressed the moral decline of the later Middle Ages. Bishops were to be responsible for preaching and instructing the people. They were to set up seminaries for the pastoral training of clergy. These seminaries trained priests who became very active in the service of the people.

Back to Basics

By way of background to understanding the re-emergence of pastoral relationship as the central aspect of pastoral care, it is necessary to refer to the movement known as the Practice of the Social Gospel. This movement influenced Protestant pastoral care during the eighteenth and nineteenth centuries.

The Practice of the Social Gospel was a response to abuses in economics and business practice, which came with the growing industrialization of the west. Some clergy were intent on correcting the abuses and striving to establish a social order that would benefit all. Washington Gladden was a principal exponent of the social gospel and he fused it with a pastoral one.[11] He attacked prevailing business practices and sought to better relationships between employers and unions.

Gladden, according to Wayne Oates, was the first to clearly define the task of pastoral care.[12] He used the term 'poimenica,' meaning the science of shepherding of souls. Gladden's pastoral care urged ecumenical pastoral calling with the various Churches co-operating with one another. The purpose of pastoral calling was to enable the pastor to promote close friendship with his flock. Gladden was convinced that pastoral relationship was the crucial factor. He preferred non-religious helpfulness and counseling. The sacraments could be used as needed or requested. He was careful to guard against superstitious practices. With Gladden, we see the re-emergence of the centrality of pastoral relationship with its emphasis on, what I call, pastoral relatedness. The primacy of this emphasis had been lost since almost the end of the second century.

The Twentieth Century Pastoral Care Movement

E. Brooks Holifield writes that the pastoral care movement of the twentieth century was the re-emergence of a trend where secular sciences are embraced to the enrichment of pastoral care.[13] The letters of St Paul reflect a pre-Christian western method of spiritual direction called 'psychagogy.' In the sixteenth century John Calvin's pastoral handbook contained many insights from medicine. In the twentieth century, pastors began to read the works of psychoanalysts such as Freud, Jung, Adler, and others. The emphasis was turning towards hearing people's private concerns in the context of pastoral relationship.

The psychological sciences, including psychiatry and psychotherapy, offered another perspective on human life and its problems, difficulties, and joys. For some, they offered an alternative perspective. However, many pastors and theological educators saw the value of integrating the insights of the sciences to develop caring pastoral relationships. Carl Rodgers' client-centered approach was adopted by many, and included the skill of active listening. At times the influence of the psychological sciences seemed to take over, but quite quickly pastoral care-givers found that their theological foundation was indispensable. The integration of the insights of the psychological sciences with the theological led to the emergence of a new discipline of pastoral care.

During the twentieth century, literature from a pastoral care perspective that applied psychoanalytic psychotherapeutic principles began to emerge. Early works were such books as *Pastoral Psychology* by Karl Stolz in 1932, and *Pastoral Psychiatry* by John Sutherland Bonnell in 1938. It is important to emphasize that the goal of pastoral care and pastoral counseling continued to have a relational focus: the relationship of care-giver and care-seeker, and the relationship of the care-seeker to self, other, and God.

This book focuses on quality pastoral care, which seeks to convey God's care to those who suffer. However, it is important to note that pastoral care practitioners do not always convey God's care. Unfortunately, some pastors abuse their privilege and engage in abusive relationships that are to the detriment of pastoral care and may damage persons' image of God.

The Twentieth Century Pastoral Care Movement in Hospitals in the USA and in Ireland

The 1920's mark a definitive time in the emergence of the modern pastoral care movement, particularly in relation to theological education for the practice of pastoral care ministry. An Episcopal physician, William S. Keller, thought that students of theology would best learn the art of pastoral care by practicing ministry with people in need and then reflecting on their efforts with experienced pastors, with a view to enhancing their practice. In 1923, Dr. Keller founded a summer school in Cincinnati, Ohio, with a view to implementing his idea.

In 1925, Richard Cabot, a neurologist and cardiologist at Worchester State Hospital, Massachusetts, published "A Plea for a Clinical Year in the Course of Theological Study." Dr. Cabot argued that theological students should be with suffering patients in hospitals and, through this experience, learn the needs of those experiencing illness. They might then apply theological learning in the practice of pastoral care.

Later, in 1925, the hospital chaplain at Worchester, Anton Boisen, initiated such a program. The theological students were exposed to long-term supervised encounters with people in crisis in hospitals, prisons, and social agencies. The students wrote case studies on some of the patients. This is the acknowledged official beginning of Clinical Pastoral Education (CPE). CPE made use of the insights of twentieth century psychology, medicine, and behavioral sciences in helping people apply their theology in clinical pastoral situations. In 1950, Boisen spoke at the twenty-fifth anniversary celebration of the beginning of clinical pastoral education. He said "Let me emphasize that this movement, as I have conceived it, has no new gospel to proclaim. We are not even seeking to introduce anything new into the theological curriculum beyond a new approach to some ancient problems . . . . What is new is the attempt to begin with the study of living human documents rather than with books, and to focus attention upon those who are grappling desperately with the issues of spiritual life and death." [14]

During the latter part of the nineteen twenties, Boisen and Cabot collaborated in supervising courses in CPE. Later they developed different approaches. The followers of Cabot emphasized the acquisition of the skills and techniques of effective communication. They were mainly chaplains in general hospitals. They formed themselves into the Institute of Pastoral Care. The followers of Boisen focused on the students gaining self-insight and understanding. They formed the Council for the Clinical Training of Theological Students. The emphases were not mutually exclusive and, after a stand off period from nineteen thirty to the mid nineteen forties, the groups became closer. They eventually merged in 1967 to form the Association of Clinical Pastoral Education (ACPE). ACPE formulated standards for the certification of hospital chaplains and supervisors of clinical pastoral education, and for the accreditation of training centers. The movement continued to grow and is now part of theological education in the United States.

After the Second Vatican Council, the Roman Catholic Church embraced the pastoral care movement. In 1965, the National Association of Catholic Chaplains (NACC) was founded in the USA. It operates standards for certification and accreditation similar to those of ACPE. Both associations certify Roman Catholic pastors.

The pastoral care movement flourished in the United States. Holifield attributes this to the influence of psychotherapy on American culture, on the network set up by the clinical pastoral educators, and on the capacity of the American economy to sustain many chaplaincy posts in hospitals and other institutions.[15]

The late nineteen seventies marked the beginning of the present emphasis on pastoral care in hospitals in Ireland. A small group of hospital chaplains, who felt the need to learn skills that would enable them to be in deeper pastoral relationship with those to whom they ministered, asked the Conference of Major Religious Superiors (CMRS), now the Conference of Religious of Ireland (CORI), to provide a training program for hospital chaplains. The result was a pilot program in Clinical Pastoral Education (CPE) in the Mater Misericordiae Hospital, Dublin in 1979, supervised by a Supervisor from the USA.

Programs supervised by Irish supervisors who had trained abroad followed. Joseph Cahill, an Irish Columban priest, supervised the first official Irish CPE program in St. Vincent's

Hospital, Elm Park, Dublin in 1981. Five CPE Centers opened in Ireland, three in Dublin, one in Cork and one in Tralee, Co. Kerry. The Association of Clinical Pastoral Education, Ireland (ACPEI) developed its own standards for the certification of supervisors and the accreditation of CPE Centers. The first generation of CPE Supervisors in Ireland is Joseph Cahill; Dermot Brennan, a Dominican priest; Norman Jennings, a Columban priest; Louise Ritchie, a religious sister of the Medical Missionaries of Mary; Una Boland, a religious sister of the Little Company of Mary; Edward Barrett, an Oblate priest; and myself. I am the first person to have trained as a CPE Supervisor in the Irish process and in accordance with the Irish standards. Tralee General Hospital, Tralee, County Kerry was the first CPE Center to undergo the ACPEI accreditation process.

Currently four CPE Centers are funded by the Irish government, through the Department of Health & Children namely, St. Vincent's Hospital, Dublin, the Mater Misericordiae Hospital, Dublin, Cork University Hospital, Cork, and Tralee General Hospital, Tralee, Co. Kerry. St. John of God Hospital, Dublin is a privately funded Center. CPE is now an integral part of healthcare chaplaincy and ministry training in Ireland.

The Person of the Pastor

The person of Jesus was central to his pastoral care. Modern pastoral care writers agree that the person of the pastor is central in modern pastoral care. The pastoral care-giver must have the ability to be in pastoral relationships that bear the quality of pastoral relatedness.[16]

David M. Taylor,[17] Kenneth H. Rogers,[18] Ernest E. Bruder,[19] Ralph D. Bonacker,[20] Blaine B. Radar, Henri Nouwen,[21] Seward Hiltner and Carroll A. Wise[22] emphasize the centrality of the person of the pastor for the creation of pastoral relationships that possess the quality of pastoral relatedness. Unless the minister possesses love, the basic Christian value, what s/he knows or does is of little value. If the pastor has Christian love, then what s/he knows and does is of immense value. Intellectual insight into human existence and deeper understanding of the nature of human beings can enrich the pastor's use of theology.

An accepting and judgement free attitude together with pastoral skills, especially the ability to listen and hear and to use religious resources, helps pastors develop pastoral relationships in which pastoral relatedness is the central quality. Such relationships contribute to the prevention and healing of illness.[23]

Blaine B. Radar researched the personality characteristics that make for effectiveness in pastoral care. Radar's research led him to question any theory that makes the exercise of pastoral care independent of the personality of the pastoral care-giver. In his Ph.D. dissertation entitled "Identification of Selected Personality Characteristics which make for Effectiveness in Pastoral Care" at Drew University in 1968, Radar advanced a two-fold hypothesis. First, effective pastoral care requires personality characteristics of its practitioner, which are empirically identifiable. Second, ecclesiastical supervisors and parishioners can discriminate superior from mediocre pastoral care-givers by means of empirical personality assessment of the pastoral care-givers. Radar's results supported the hypotheses. Effective pastoral characteristics of care workers possess good mental health. They are mature people with insight into their own and others' behavior. They possess a sense of personal worth and freedom. They are lower in aggression, are focused towards the personal, and they endorse non-coercive assistance of other people.

Developing the concept of the centrality of the person of the pastor, Barry Estadt and William J. Moorman list the qualities of a pastoral counselor.[24] S/he is a religiously integrated person, approaches the other with a sense of mystery, has the ability to communicate with the other in a therapeutic relationship, and strives to bring the other to reconciliation and personal religious integration. The pastoral counselor possesses a body of knowledge about counseling theory and practice, has developed counseling skills, possesses an understanding of persons and therapeutic processes and of his/her own role as minister.

Henri Nouwen writes that those with good self-esteem have the ability to 'be with.' Their concern for others is motivated more by the need of the other than by self-need. Those whose self-esteem is low have a desire and need to be doing. Their self-need is greater than the need of the other.

Chris R. Schlauch outlines a style of pastoral response, which originates in introspection and empathy.[25] In this style the pastor gives careful attention to his/her own inner experience, so as to be keenly aware of his/her thoughts and feelings. As well as being self-consciously aware of his/her own thoughts and feelings, the pastor prepares for giving pastoral care by paying careful attention to what the thoughts and feelings of the other might be. In this way the care-giver monitors the experience of the other as if s/he were the other. This is empathy or 'vicarious introspection.'[26] Out of this model the care-giver is 'with' the other and responds accurately to the other. Schlauch places much importance on 'being with.' In a footnote, he confesses his fondness for the phrase: "Don't just do something, stand there!" [27]

The pastor, by attitude and action, attempts to convey the care and concern of God, of the church, of the Christian community, and ultimately of Jesus Christ. S/he attempts to help people meet their need for intimacy with God and journeys with them in their search for meaning. The hospital chaplain helps to meet people's psychological need for care, comfort, support, and companionship, specifically in the context of the Christian community in the hospital and, more generally, in the context of the whole Christian community. To achieve these goals, the chaplain must be aware of his/her strengths and weaknesses in ministry. This enables him/her to be in pastoral relationship with another person in a way that communicates God to the person to whom s/he ministers.

Notes

1. G. H. Tucker, "Old Testament and Apocrypha, Traditions and theology of Care In," in *Dictionary of Pastoral Care and Counseling*, ed. Rodney J. Hunter (Nashville: Abingdon Press, 1990), 799.
2. A.J. Malherbe, "New Testament, Traditions and the Theology of Care in," in *Dictionary of Pastoral Care and Counseling*, 787-792.
3. Blaine B. Radar, "Identification of Selected Personality Characteristics which make for Effectiveness in Pastoral Care" (Ph.D. diss. Drew University, 1968), 10-15.
4. J.I.H. McDonald, "The New Testament and Pastoral Care," in *A Dictionary of Pastoral Care*, ed. Alastair V. Campbell (London: SPCK, 1987), 172-174.
5. L.O. Mills, "Pastoral Care (History, Traditions and Definitions), in *Dictionary of Pastoral Care and Counseling*, 836-44.
6. W. H. C. Frend, "Pastoral Care: History-The Early Church," in *A Dictionary of Pastoral Care*, 190-2.
7. J. D. Creighton, "Pastoral Care: History-The Roman Catholic Tradition," in *A Dictionary of Pastoral Care*, 195-6.

8. Blaine B. Radar, 10-98.
9. W.H.C. Frend, "Pastoral Care: History–The Early Church," 191.
10. Carter Lindberg, "The Lutheran Tradition," 173-99; in Ronald L. Numbers and David W. Amundsen, eds., *Caring and Curing: Health and Medicine in the Western Religious Traditions* (New York: MacMillan Publishing Co., 1986), 182. Borrowed from John T. McNeill, *A History of the Cure of Souls* (New York, n. p. 1951), 163.
11. Washington Gladden (1836-1918), a Congregational pastor in Columbus, Ohio, USA.
12. Blaine B. Radar, 55. Wayne E. Oates is a twentieth century American Protestant pastoral theologian.
13. E.B. Holifield, "Pastoral Care Movement," in *Dictionary of Pastoral Care and Counseling*, 846.
14. Association of Clinical Pastoral Education, "CPE - 50 Years – Learning with Living Human Documents," News, 8 no. 1 (1975): 5. Don S. Browning's approach, outlined at the beginning of Chapter 1 advances this.
15. E. B. Holifield, 849.
16. Ward Knights and David Kramer, writing in 1964 refer an article by Edward S. Golden in which Golden notes that the personality of the chaplain is a significant variable in the evaluation of chaplaincy services. The article is "What Influences the Role of the Protestant Chaplain in an Institutional Setting?" *The Journal of Pastoral Care* 16 no. 4 (1962): 218-25. Knights and Kramer's article is "Chaplaincy Role-Functions as seen by Mental Patients and Staff," *The Journal of Pastoral Care*, 18 no. 3 (1964): 154-60.
17. David M. Taylor, "Clinical Pastoral Training," *The Journal of Pastoral Care* 16 no. 1 (1962): 36.
18. Kenneth H. Rogers, "Preparation for an Effective Pastoral Ministry," *The Journal of Pastoral Care* 10 no. 3 (1956): 161-9.
19. Ernest E. Bruder, "Clinical Pastoral Training in Preparation for Pastoral Ministry," *The Journal of Pastoral Care* 16 no.1 (1962): 25-33.
20. Ralph D. Bonacker, "Clinical Training for Pastoral Ministry: Purposes and Methods," *The Journal of Pastoral Care* 14 no.1 (1960): 1-12.
21. Henri Nouwen, *Out of Solitude* (Notre Dame, Indiana: Ave Maria Press, 1974), passim.
22. Seward Hiltner and Carroll A. Wise are twentieth century American Protestant pastoral theologians.
23. Illness means the whole experience of being sick, physical, emotional, social and spiritual; disease is the physical component of illness.
24. Estadt, Barry, and William J. Moorman. "Pastoral Counseling in the Health Care Setting." In *Health Care Ministry: A Handbook for Chaplains*, eds. Helen Hayes and Cornelius J. van der Poel, 170-85. New York: Paulist Press, 1990.
25. Chris R. Schlauch, "Expanding the Contexts of Pastoral Care," *The Journal of Pastoral Care* 44 no. 4 (1990): 359-371.
26. Heinz Kohut is the author of this phrase. It is discussed in "Introspection, Empathy and Psychoanalysis: An Examination of the Relationship Mode of Observation and Theory," in Kohut's *The Search for Self* (New York, NY: International Universities Press, 1978), p.206.
27. Ibid., 368.

Chapter 2

The Theology of Pastoral Care

No one person has the fullness of wisdom. Different theologians have developed theologies of pastoral care. A study of the theologies of pastoral care of representative Protestant and Roman Catholic theologians reveals recurring themes namely, love, ultimate concern, service, shepherding, and the proclamation of the Word, who is Jesus Christ. This chapter considers the theologies of pastoral care of representative Protestant and Roman Catholic theologians. More has been written within the Protestant tradition, where the modern pastoral care movement has a longer history. Within the Protestant tradition, theologies of pastoral care are represented by theologians including Alastair V. Campbell, David Belgum, Paul E. Johnson, William A. Clebsch and Charles R. Jackle, Paul Tillich, Wayne E. Oates, Carroll A. Wise, Seward Hiltner, Edward Thurneysen,[1] Howard Clinebell, and Howard Stone.[2]

Love is the starting point for Campbell, Belgum, and Johnson. Clebsch and Jackle, and Tillich theologize pastoral care in the context of ultimate concern, though each has a different emphasis on how pastoral care is practiced. The themes of service and shepherding dominate the theologies of Hiltner and Thurneysen, while Stone argues that the essence of pastoral care is the proclamation of the word of God, who is Christ.

Within the Roman Catholic tradition are the theologies of Walter J. Burghardt and Robert L. Kinast, based on the concepts of 'being sent' and liberation respectively.

Theologies of Pastoral Care of Representative Protestant Theologians

Love is the foundation for one group of Protestant theologians including Alastair V. Campbell, David Belgum, and Paul E. Johnson. Alastair V. Campbell sees pastoral care as based on love.[3] Love is the great commandment, "You must love the Lord your God with all your heart, with all your soul, with all your strength, and with all your mind, and you must love your neighbor as yourself" (Lk. 10:27 JB). This love must extend to all people. The Parable of the Good Samaritan clarifies that neighbor is anyone who is in need (Lk. 10: 25-37). Common humanity and common human experience unite persons. In love, they respond to one another's needs in the context of relationship with God and ultimate meaning and concerns. This concerns the well-being of individuals and of community.

David Belgum's theology is that pastoral care is the love and grace of God conveyed to another under special stress or in particular need.[4] We love and care for others because God loved and cared for us first (I Jn. 4: 19). Love is the basis of all pastoral care. It permeates all its activities. In pastoral relationships, the pastoral care-giver conveys the love and grace of God. It is the task of the pastoral care-giver to remove whatever makes the operation of grace more difficult, whether this is a spiritual, emotional, social, or physical factor. The pastoral care-giver does so by helping the person muster his/her resources and strengths. During the Middle Ages, the representative of the Church often did so by practicing medical science. In the twentieth century, the pastor often utilizes the insights of the psychological and social sciences. In this way these sciences interface with theology in the theory and practice of pastoral care. For Belgum "pastoral care is a natural expression of theology."[5]

Paul E. Johnson defines pastoral care as "the faithful ministry of a religious community to the needs of persons in face-to-face relationships."[6] This care arises from genuine concern for another. Johnson again emphasizes that pastoral care must spring from a definite theology. Love is the foundation, beginning with God's love for people revealed throughout the history of salvation. We are called to continue this work of love by word and deed. "As the Father has loved me, so I have loved you. Remain in my love." (Jn. 15:9-10 JB). "Love one another as I have loved you" (Jn. 15:12 JB). This demands that we are to care for one another in accordance with the uniqueness of our gifts. God is present in the loving pastoral relationship, in the caring community of love. Johnson stresses the importance of teamwork in pastoral care. The pastor's role includes assisting the laity to be pastoral care-givers.

Another group of theologians shares theology themes including William A. Clebsch and Charles R. Jaekle, Paul Tillich, Edward Thurneysen, Seward Hiltner, and Howard Stone. Clebsch and Jaekle consider pastoral care to be in the realm of ultimate concern and meaning and to consist of 'helping acts' by pastors who strive to heal, sustain, guide, and reconcile troubled persons.[7] Healing restores the person to a new level of spiritual wholeness. Sustaining helps hurting persons to endure and transcend a circumstance that is unalterable. Guiding helps persons to make informed choices. Reconciling seeks to restore broken relationships with God and with others. These authors suggest that the distinctive quality of pastoral care is its being offered by a Christian person. Pastoral Care is to assist an individual person rather than be for the service of the Church or a group. Wayne E. Oates also argues for pastoral care to take its direction from helping people in crisis.[8] This help may take the form of friendship, comfort, confession, teaching, or pastoral counseling. For Carroll A. Wise the nature of pastoral care includes both whatever is gained from helpful acts and the insight gained from pastoral counseling.[9] Wise also stresses the vital importance of the kind of person the pastor is, rather than what the pastor does.

Paul Tillich sees person as ultimately concerned.[10] That, for Tillich, is faith. All other concerns are secondary to ultimate concern. The whole of creation, including person, is not fully integrated or in a state of total well-being. Anxiety and threat exist and are always on the horizon.[11] There is always need of healing. Salvation is being totally integrated, whole, and healed. The source of healing is in the transcendent. Persons participate in the transcendent by way of symbols. Religious symbols do not make the transcendent immanent, but they do represent the transcendent. Any integration and healing achieved in the immanent realm is achieved through symbolic participation in the transcendent and represents ultimate integration, wholeness, and healing.

As such, persons cannot avoid being involved in care. Every person is a care-giver or pastor to another at some level, though this may be exercised indirectly or even unconsciously. The aim of care is the fulfillment of human potentialities and integration. The professional care-giver exercises caring in a conscious way. The uniqueness of pastoral care is that its work is in the dimension of ultimate concern. The central function of Tillich's pastoral care is the promotion of acceptance, which mirrors the acceptance by the transcendent of the finitude of humanity. Pastoral care is characterized by mutuality, as both pastor and patient are in the power of the transcendent. The pastor must be aware of this if s/he is to be of assistance to the patient. The person of the pastor is of the utmost importance.

Thurneysen and Hiltner emphasize the primacy of service and shepherding. For Thurneysen pastoral care is a way to, and at the service of, the Word and the sacraments.[12] The pastoral conversation can help lead the person to hear the Word and receive the sacraments. That is its sole function and that is why it is necessary. Pastoral care can help lead the sinner to reconciliation and forgiveness. Hence, for Thurneysen, pastoral care is located only within the Church. Thurneysen regards psychology and psychotherapy, with their knowledge of persons, as indispensable in the work of pastoral care. Theologically, he accepts the priesthood of all believers and hence that pastoral care is the responsibility of all the faithful, but asserts that some are called by the Holy Spirit to devote themselves fully to the task of pastoral care.

Seward Hiltner's theology of pastoral care begins with role of the Protestant pastoral minister. S/he is to communicate the Word, to organize the community to be one of Christian fellowship and to shepherd the flock, especially those in trouble, with a caring attitude. Pastoral care is mainly in the realm of shepherding. Hiltner also raises the question of the person of the pastoral care-giver. He states that the most important requirement for pastoral care is the pastoral care-giver's self-understanding. The pastoral care-giver must possess a full understanding of the Christian tradition.

Hiltner cites that there are three aspects of pastoral care, healing, sustaining, and guiding. Hiltner's concept of healing is in the context of sin and salvation. Considering 'sin' in the generic sense, Hiltner regards sin as a lack of wholeness. Wholeness is only achievable by the healing of God. Disease, distortion, and defects are manifestations of sin in the world. The healing of a troubled person in pastoral care is movement towards complete wholeness. Healing generates hope. Sustaining is mainly 'being with' another in the other's suffering. It is often exercised in crisis, maybe shock or loss, and in journeying with a person in an unchangeable process. Hiltner sees the work of pastoral care in these situations as calling forth hope and helping a person move forward in terms of attitude. Guiding involves leading a person so that the person can utilize the resources s/he possesses. It may also include helping the person make a decision and/or clarifying alternatives for the person.

Howard Clinebell's theology of pastoral care focuses on supporting, being adaptive, and reality orientated, as opposed to exploring depth and searching for insights. He focuses more on coping with the present and planning for the future rather than exploring the past. Clinebell also emphasizes responsibility, utilizing a person's strengths and reducing negative factors, evaluating behavior, and most importantly, ministering in the context of a person's relationship with God.

Finally, in more recent times and in his essay "The Word of God and Pastoral Care," Howard Stone argues that the essence of pastoral care (and of ministry) is the proclamation of the word of God, who is Christ.[13] Ministry is broader than pastoral care. Ministry is every way the word of God is proclaimed, including preaching, teaching, liturgy, and pastoral care.

God reveals God's self in Christ. In Christ, God communicates God's self verbally and visibly. In Christ we meet God, who calls us to intimate relationship. In pastoral care, God is communicated in various ways verbally and visibly in the context of this relationship. God is communicated visibly in and through presence and gestures. God is communicated verbally in and through the spoken word. Relationship involves listening and sharing.[14]

For Stone, the purpose and essence of pastoral care is to communicate God in the context of a warm pastoral relationship.

Previously the practice of pastoral care emphasized the verbal word, offering guidance and providing explanations and answers to people's questions. With the growth of psychotherapy in the 1940's and 1950's, the pendulum swung to the other extreme with emphasis on non-directive counseling and on the ministry of presence. Stone, agreeing with Charles Gerkin, argues that a balance between these extremes is integral and true pastoral care.

For Stone, every human concern that the pastor encounters in pastoral care is seen as having a relationship with God's word. God's word is in every human experience. A pastoral conversation proceeds from the word of God and intends to lead to the word of God. It involves actively listening to human concerns and problems in the light of the word. Pastoral care believes that the word of God is important for these concerns and problems, whether it is with a listening ear, affirming a person's personhood, or in sacrament. In whatever way, God is there. God's word is communicated, not by the pastoral care-giver, but through the Holy Spirit's transformation of the pastoral care encounter. Stone agrees with John B. Cobb, Jr.,[15] that the pastoral care person transmits God's word, who is Christ, through the Holy Spirit.

The first task is to establish the care relationship. The skills of psychotherapy enable this. Within this relationship the word of God is communicated differently by different people, but striving always to do so as is appropriate for the particular relationship and encounter. It may be in 'being with' or pastoral relatedness, bringing a word of peace, hope, confrontation, or challenge.

Roman Catholic Pastoral Care Themes and Theologies of Pastoral Care of Representative Roman Catholic Theologians

The Second Vatican Council initiated a profound shift in Roman Catholic thinking, which had a major impact on Roman Catholic pastoral care. This section outlines this change and considers the theologies of pastoral care of Walter J. Burghardt and Robert L. Kinast. Bughardt's theology of pastoral care is based on 'being sent.' Kinast develops the concept of liberation in terms of pastoral care.

The Second Vatican Council

The Roman Catholic Church resisted change until the mid nineteen sixties. In 1959, Pope John XXIII called the Second Vatican Council. It was to be a pastoral council. Vatican II opened the doors for pastoral development. The Roman Catholic Church embraced the new understanding of ways of ministering to people suffering life's difficulties of illness, death, bereavement, divorce, family conflict, and other pastoral and moral issues. Previously, in the 1950's, some Roman Catholic priests had studied psychology, but did not integrate it with their theology. They studied it as a person would study a science such as physics or mathematics. Many of these priests began to realize that the insights of psychology, which helped them to understand people, could be integrated into their ministry.

Vatican II had a profound effect. The Church is the people of God. The emphasis on the priesthood of all Christians by virtue of their baptism re-emerged. The attitude of openness allowed psychology to influence and be integrated in pastoral care. After some years the notion that people other than ordained ministers could be ministers and pastors was accepted. Many lay people took courses in pastoral care and pastoral counseling, and later in theology. The declining number of vocations to the ordained priesthood led to openings for lay women and men in pastoral care and counseling, initially in the United States. Pastoral care came to be defined in ways similar to the definition used in this book. A number of the documents of Vatican II emphasize that clergy and laity co-operate and are co-responsible for a holistic pastoral care service.[16] However, the ordained priesthood in the Roman Catholic Church is confined to men and leading of the celebration of the sacraments is confined to ordained priests.

As the years pass, the fusion of theology and psychology deepens. Pastoral care continues its commitment to fostering people's relationship with God and helping people find peace and meaning in life.

Themes in Roman Catholic Pastoral Care[17]

Pastoral care exists in order to continue the ministry of Jesus. Jesus came to inaugurate the Kingdom of God in the world. But Jesus' mission is not yet complete. Pastoral care and pastoral counseling are part of the Church's work of continuing the mission of Jesus to proclaim the reign of God and to work towards 'the realization of the Kingdom of God' in the world. Pastoral counseling removes impediments so people can emotionally and spiritually 'see, walk, and hear.' In Roman Catholic theology, the pastor's mission is 'to serve Christ.' It is vocation for Christ's sake only.

Roman Catholic pastoral care is 'incarnational.' It makes God present through the sacraments and through pastoral relationships. The purpose of all pastoral care is ultimately to aid the person towards 'eternal salvation.' Pastoral care and pastoral counseling are to remove blocks, which may hinder a person's journey towards salvation.

These blocks are mainly in relationships with God and with others. Roman Catholic theology stresses the concept of the 'Church as community,' and Roman Catholic pastoral care is situated in the context of the 'Church as community.'

Another theme in the Roman Catholic theology of pastoral care is that of 'Redemptive Suffering.' Somehow meaning can be found in suffering if the person seeks meaning. For example, it may help a person be a more compassionate helper to others.

Theologies of Pastoral Care of Representative Roman Catholic Theologians

Walter J. Burghardt SJ offers a theology of pastoral care based on 'being sent.'[18] God reached out to humanity and sent Jesus into the world so that the world might have life to the full. The Father and the Son sent the Holy Spirit to the Church to sanctify it.

The Church is sent by the Son in the Spirit to reach out to people. The sending came after Jesus' resurrection: "As the Father sent me, so am I sending you" (Jn. 20:21 JB). The Church is people. Jesus sent people to convey the Good News of God and to serve one another as God's People, removing obstacles to redemption.

The care-giver must be motivated by love, if pastoral care is to be personal. The care-giver must be in a relationship of love in Christ with the other person. In this pastoral relationship God meets the human person as s/he works out his/her salvation. Burchardt emphasizes the need to do this in the human situation, in helping the hungry person be fed and the sick person be healed. In this way, the care-giver prepares the way for a genuinely human existence for the other so that redemption can touch that person. At some time we have to face the ultimate mystery, which is death. For the Christian, death is a 'yes' to life.

Burghardt and David Belgum, one of the Protestant theologians considered earlier, have similar theologies of pastoral care. Both stress the care of God being conveyed to the other through the practice of pastoral care. In the practical situation both see pastoral care as striving to remove blocks in a stressful situation. Burchardt calls it removing the obstacles to redemption. Belgum calls it removing whatever makes the operation of God's grace more difficult. Both stress that the most important aspect of pastoral care is personal pastoral relationship. It is through such a relationship that the blocks are removed and grace is allowed to flow more freely.

Robert L. Kinast is a Roman Catholic theologian, whose theology of pastoral care is based on the concept of liberation.[19] In Christ, God initiated God's covenant with us so that we might be free. "It was for freedom that Christ set us free" (Gal. 5:1 NAB). The Church cares for God's covenant when it liberates people. This liberating action is the Church's ministry, which continues the ministry of Jesus. Pastoral care is an aspect of this ministry.

The exercise of the Church's ministry is on three levels, the intrapersonal, the interpersonal, and the communal-societal. The intrapersonal is the uniqueness of each person, the deepest level of mystery in each person. The interpersonal is the area of deep and rich shared human experiences. The communal-societal is the area of groupings in which people live, and in society as a whole. Any or all areas may be lacking in freedom. The freeing of the block is liberating. Jesus ministered at all levels. The gospels portray him ministering to individuals on many occasions, but he ministered in the wider level also.

Kinast sees the scope of pastoral care as all the members of the faith community offering care to one another. The hospital chaplain and the parish pastor have a significant role in pastoral care in that these persons exemplify in a concentrated and a public way the pastoral care that is happening in the whole faith community.

Pastoral care has a healing function. Healing has different aspects, spiritual, psychological, and physical. Kinast sees spiritual healing as healing that "confronts sin and seeks sainthood." It is mainly in the intrapersonal area but overlaps into the other areas. Pastoral care is holistic, though its primary concern is in the spiritual dimension. It is not possible to separate the different aspects. All impinge on each other.

For Kinast, pastoral care includes a liberating response by a church member to a person in trouble, utilizing the person's inner resources and those of the Church to help integrate the person with the faith community. Liberation enables a person to feel in charge of his/her most intimate self, where God is most present. The pastoral care-giver's skills help enable persons to own and utilize their strengths, and those of the Church, to facilitate healing. As a result, the person is more integrated and the whole Church is more integrated. Kinast's theology, in keeping with Roman Catholic theology, views any person's growth within the Church as enhancing the experience of the whole Church, as it continues the care of Jesus.

My Personal Theology of Pastoral Care

One of the questions that prompted this work concerns how my life and work as a pastoral care-giver is grounded in theological meaning. The pastor's inspiration and motivation to care is inspired by and has meaning in the pastor's relationship with God, which is based on the spiritual value of love. It is important that a pastoral care-giver possess a theological foundation, which integrates theology with everyday life and ministry. A Christian pastoral care-giver must have a firm faith in the Triune God as revealed in Jesus Christ in the love of the Spirit to sustain him/herself in the midst of existential crises; hence the importance of a theological grounding to sustain one's ongoing work as a pastoral care-giver. Developing my own theology of pastoral care enables me to make a connection, which sustains me, between academic theology and my everyday life work as a pastoral care-giver.

Reflection on pastoral experience and the various theologies of pastoral care has led me to a summary statement of my theology of pastoral care. The love of God, revealed in Jesus Christ and with us through the Holy Spirit, motivates a pastoral care-giver to reach out to people, and through the medium of pastoral relatedness, the pastor communicates God's love to those who suffer. This enables the person to remove blocks in relating to God and others, and thus experience the freedom of the Son of God and move towards salvation.

Notes:

1. Edward Thurneysen, a minister of the Reformed Cathedral in Basel and a co-worker of theologian, Karl Barth.
2. Tillich, Clinebell, Clebsch and Jaekle, Campbell, Belgum, Johnson, and Stone are twentieth century American Protestant pastoral theologians.
3. Alastair V. Campbell, "Pastoral Care, Nature of," in *A Dictionary of Pastoral Care*, (London, SPCK, 1987), 188-90.
4. David Belgum, "The Theology of Pastoral Care," *The Lutheran Quarterly*, 11 no. 3 (1959): 207-21.
5. Ibid., 208.
6. Paul E. Johnson, "A Theology of Pastoral Care," *Journal of Religion and Health* 3 no. 2 (1964): 171.
7. Blaine B. Radar, 89-90.
8. Ibid., 91-2.
9. Ibid., 93-4.

10. Paul Tillich, "The Theology of Pastoral Care," *Pastoral Psychology* 10 no. 9 (1959): 22.

11. Donald W. Shriver, Jr. notes that Tillich considered death to be the major anxiety of the ancient Graeco-Roman world, sin as the major anxiety of the medieval European world, and anxiety about meaning in life as the major anxiety of the modern world. Donald W. Schriver, ed. *Medicine and Religion: Strategies for Care* (Pittsburgh: University of Pittsburgh, 1980), 9.

12. Blaine B. Radar, 62-71.

13. Howard Stone, "The Word of God and Pastoral Care," *Encounter* 44 no. 4 (1983): 369-90.

14. Charles Gerkin, *Crisis Experience in Modern Life* (Nashville: Abingdon Press, 1979), 15-6; quoted in Howard Stone, "The Word of God and Pastoral Care," 379.

15. John B. Cobb, Jr., *Theology and Pastoral Care* (Philadelphia: Fortress Press, 1977), 52; quoted in Howard Stone, "The Word of God and Pastoral Care" 381.

16. These documents are "Dogmatic Constitution on the Church;" "Decree on the Bishops' Pastoral Office in the Church;" "Decree on the Apostolate of the Laity;" and "Decree on the Ministry and Life of Priests," *The Documents of Vatican II: All Sixteen Official Texts Promulgated By The Ecumenical Council* 1963-1965 (London, Geoffrey Chapman, 1966), 107-32, 389-433, 486-525, 526-79.

17. For this section I am indebted to Br. Kevin Kriso for his D. Min. term paper, "A Roman Catholic Perspective on Pastoral Care and Counseling" (Boston University, 1996), 11-20.

18. Walter J. Burghardt, "Towards A Theology of Pastoral Care," (n.p.:n.d.), 1-8.

19. Robert L. Kinast, "Caring for God's Covenant of Freedom: A Theology of Pastoral Care," in *Health Care Ministry: A Handbook for Chaplains*, eds. Helen Hayes and Cornelius J. van der Poel (New York: Paulist Press, 1990), 7-21.

Chapter 3

How can the Transcendent God be Caring?

Christian theology has always emphasized how close God is to each person, while also declaring that God is transcendent. But how can a transcendent God 'be with' a person in his/her suffering? Christian theologians have discussed this question in the context of the doctrine of the Trinity, which considers the relationships within the Triune God. Among the theologians, who have demonstrated how God is with each person in a close caring relationship are the major theologian of the Middle Ages, St. Thomas Aquinas(1225-74), and twentieth century theologians, American Lee E. Snook, professor at Lutheran-Northwestern Theological Seminaries in St. Paul, MN, and the German theologian, Jurgen Moltmann. The transcendent God is caring in 'being with' the other.

St. Thomas Aquinas. St. Thomas Aquinas states that language is limited in describing God. Knowledge of God is limited because the essence of God is beyond the limits of our minds.

Aquinas began his consideration by looking at people, the effects of God's creation, "the creatures that tell the glory of the creator."[1] For Aquinas, because God is in intimate relationship with creatures, creatures can point beyond themselves to the transcendence of God, to God as their ultimate cause. This can only be if God is beyond the order of creatures. God is immanent because God is transcendent. To reduce God to the order of creatures would be to diminish God's intimate presence. God, as the cause of all being, is closer to each person than that person is to self. And it is as Triune God that God, through the missions of the Son and the Spirit, is present to each person in this way. This presence is of the nature of God.

Michael J. Dodds, reflecting on Aquinas' theology, sees the intimate unity of the Triune God in the graciousness of love, in communion between people, and in compassion. The graciousness of love is love's concern for the good of the other. Any act of human love no matter how good is never completely gratuitous because it is our human nature to seek self-fulfillment. There will always be some degree of self-seeking in a person's efforts. Only a transcendent God could be perfectly gratuitous. God can be this intimate with each person. We can be sure that the Son's redemptive act of love on the cross is of the infinite gratuity of God.

There can never be complete and perfect unity in communion between people. There is always room for further growth or depth. This is part of human finitude. Communion with God is not subject to these human limitations. As there is complete unity in the Trinity, "The Father and I are one" (Jn. 10:30 JB), God is in complete union with each person. The divine persons of the Trinity are fully relational, while human persons are partially relational. In God's love persons are somehow brought into this divine relationship with the same love with which God loves the Son, the love who is the Spirit.

Compassion means suffering with the other in order to relieve the suffering of the other. In human compassion there is always some element of sadness in the person being compassionate. When a person acts to relieve the suffering of another s/he is, to some extent, acting to relieve his/her own distress. Jesus, as human and divine, is able to be totally compassionate with the other. In Matthew 25 he says, "I was sick ..." (Mt. 25:36 JB). He doesn't say "You were sick and it saddened me." Compassion also involves seeking to relieve the distress of the other. As pastors, we witness much suffering. Why is this if God is compassionate? The only answer is in the Cross, which proclaims God's presence in our suffering. However, this is not a passive presence but an active presence of hope. In this way, without being subject to it, God is intimately present with a person who is suffering. God is more intimately present than that person is with him or herself. God's graciousness, God's communion with us, and God's compassion are the keys to thinking about Aquinas' theology of the Trinity as a reflection of pastoral relatedness in a pastoral relationship. Gratuitousness surely includes love, sincerity, closeness, acceptance, and freedom. Communion in love must include trust, judgement-free attitude, honesty, closeness, capacity to create the atmosphere in which a person feels able to disclose what is innermost or intimate. This is 'being-with.' Compassion includes 'being-with' and conveying hope.

In the human situation we are always less than perfect. God in us and with us relates to us with perfect intimacy and immanence. This is because of God's transcendence. However we can, in God, strive towards perfection in pastoral relationships. In this way we can make God's presence and relatedness with each person more tangible as we continue the work of Jesus in the Spirit.

Lee E. Snook. Lee E. Snook, in reflecting on relationships and the Trinity, aims to bridge the gap between the academic study of theology and day-to-day realities of Christian living. Considering the doctrine of the Trinity, he attempts to do so in terms of his close relationships with his four children. My consideration of Snook's theology focuses on two questions. First, why the threefoldness of the Trinity? Second, how are relationships within this threefoldness connected to relationships in our lives?

The doctrine of the Trinity is an attempt to express in doctrine the lived experience and faith of those who encountered Jesus in the world. The New Testament writers experienced Jesus, in his life, death and resurrection, as the reality of God in the world. They believed in him as evidence of God's will to free people from death. They put their trust in God revealed in Jesus. The story cannot be told without reference to both God and Jesus.

Why the threefoldness if the Christian experience is in the relationship? Snook's theology is based on love. There is one God in threefoldness. Jesus revealed God's desire for a love relationship with every person. This love relationship is enabled and enlivened by God's Holy Spirit. Thus, there is one God in threefoldness. The Father, the Son, and the Spirit are one and cannot be dissociated.

As Aquinas did, Snook also declares that any effort to convey lived experience that is beyond language is inadequate. The doctrine of the Trinity, arrived at after many years of thinking following Jesus' life, death and resurrection, is the best attempt to date to convey the faith of the early Christians in words and concepts. The concept of holism is helpful to me in my efforts to conceptualize the Jesus experience of the early Christians.

That first question is by way of background to the second question, how are relationships within this threefoldness connected to relationships in our lives? Snook uses the concept of 'relatedness' to describe the relationships within the Trinity. He is at pains to convey that this means "intimate, not remote; internal, not external."[3] He views the relationships within the Trinity as "a kind of definition and disclosure" of his close relationships with his children. This logic of relatedness allows people the freedom to belong, to really 'be-with.' Really 'being-with' necessarily possesses the quality of pastoral relatedness, as I have defined it.

This concept is further clarified in relation to suffering.[4] Since the life, death and resurrection of Jesus is God's way of being and living in the world, God's will to be Lover makes God vulnerable to suffering. The assurance that God's resolve to love will not break is that God suffered the death of God's own Son. The doctrine of the Trinity means that salvation is not from suffering, but through suffering, with God as Lover and Companion in suffering. This is God 'being-with.' A pastor who can 'be with' a person who is suffering, in a relationship of pastoral relatedness, is truly a bearer of God's grace.

Snook believes that the Trinity reveals "the deepest nature of human relationships."[5] He agrees with Karl Rahner that relation cannot be adequately defined independently of Trinity.[6]

Jürgen Moltmann. Jürgen Moltmann's theology of the Trinity is centered on the Cross as Trinitarian event.[7] Jesus died as an outsider, outside the city gates, lowly, despised, and abandoned by some of his disciples and by God. He was Godforsaken. God was silent when Jesus prayed "Abba Father, everything is possible for you. Take this cup away from me" (Mk. 14:35 JB), and when Jesus cried from the cross, "My God, my God, why have you deserted me?" (Mk. 15:34 JB). Two consequences of the Cross event are that the Cross informs the meaning of the Resurrection and that the Cross was a Trinitarian event in God. First, the Cross informs the meaning of the Resurrection. To quote Moltmann: "The new and scandalous element in the Christian message of Easter was not that some man or other was raised before anyone else, but that the one who was raised was this condemned, executed and forsaken man."[8] Jesus was raised as the abandoned and forsaken One. This means that God does not abandon the abandoned. Second, Jesus' forsakenness means that the Cross was a Trinitarian event in God. God the Father forsook God the Son. God the Son suffered the pain in the garden and on the Cross. God the Father suffered the death of the Son, suffered the grief of love. Yet the Father and Son were still bound together in the love of the Spirit. Jesus' forsakenness and death are part of the history of God. Jesus' death becomes an event in God. Christianity depends on the resurrection of this Jesus from the dead. The resurrection of Jesus is the eschatological hope for all. It is a definite and concrete hope.

Thinking about pastoral relationships in terms of these relationships, it is not difficult for me to deduce the quality of pastoral relatedness. God does not abandon the abandoned. Surely this suggests a deep level of love, trust, commitment, sincerity, fidelity, and warmth.

The death of Jesus was an event in God. All the time the Father and Son were bound together in the love of the Spirit, even when it was not apparent that the seemingly abandoned one would be rescued from the finality of death. All the time, in the love of the Spirit, the qualities of compassion and 'being with' were present. Inevitably, this contains hope.

Moltmann's theology is that the Cross as Trinitarian event is the ultimate revelation of the transcendent as well the immanent trinitarian life of God. The Cross was an event between the Father, Son, and Spirit. Moltmann begins with the Trinity and seeks to establish the unity of God rather than beginning with the unity of God and developing towards the Triune God. For Moltmann, God's unity is essentially that of community. Surely this informs the community of the pastor and person in pastoral relationship.

Lawrence E. Henning, in analyzing Moltmann's theology in relation to pastoral care, stresses that "The Cross means that Jesus stands in solidarity with those who suffer."[9] There is no outside the gate, no godforsakenness now. The Resurrection has happened. No pain or suffering can separate us from the love of God revealed by the Cross. The Resurrection means that there is hope for the future. The trinitarian event of the Cross has a dual focus - sharing the darkness, and struggling to experience the light. Moltmann wrote, "every act of caring has its origin in Christian fellowship. Before you can be for others, you must be with others."[10] Pastoral Relatedness seeks to communicate this sharing of darkness and struggle so that people will experience the light of God's care. The people to whom we minister are fellows in the community of the Trinity - "I was sick and you visited me" (Mk. 25:36 JB). The Cross as Trinitarian event commands us to develop, and to help others develop, the capacity for relatedness in pastoral relationships.

In pastoral relationships the transcendent God is experienced in an immanent way. These relationships are incarnational and thus revelatory. Sr. Mary Paul Cutri calls it "the touch of God."[11] It facilitates deeper intimacy between the other and the Other.

Notes:

1. Michael J. Dodds, "Ultimacy and Intimacy. Aquinas on the Relation between God and the World," in *Ordo Sapientiae et Amoris*, ed. Carlos-Josephet Pinto de Oliveira, (Fribourg Suisse: Editions Universitaires, 1993), 213.
2. Lee E. Snook, "A Primer on the Trinity: Keeping Our Theology Christian," *Word and World* 2 no. 1 (1982).
3. Ibid., 6.
4. Ibid., 14-5.
5. Ibid., 6.
6. Ibid., 6, footnote 3.

7. Lawrence H. Henning, "The Cross and Pastoral Care," *Currents in Theology and Mission* 13 no. 1 (1986).

8. Jurgen Moltmann, *The Crucified God* (New York: Harper and Row, 1974), 175; quoted in Lawrence H. Henning, "The Cross and Pastoral Care," 24.

9. Ibid., 24.

10. Jurgen Moltmann. "The Diaconal Church in the Context of the Kingdom of God," in Hope for the Church (Nashville: Abingdon Press, 1979), 25; quoted in Lawrence Henning, "The Cross and Pastoral Care," 26.

11. Sr. Mary Paul Cutri, "The Touch of God: Human/Divine Intimacy," *Spiritual Life* 30 (fall 1984): 155.

Chapter 4

Experiencing the Touch of God

Psychologists have considered how a person is close to his/her spiritual self. This chapter considers how this is effected in the context of a pastoral relationship. This links the theology and psychology in that for the believer, God is experienced in the person's deep, inner, spiritual self; in the core of his/her being. Here God and the person embrace one another. For this to happen, a person must access this inner core of self. This may be enabled within a pastoral relationship that possesses the quality of pastoral relatedness. Theology and psychology are linked in that the pastoral relationship enables psychological and spiritual healing.

How does a person experience the 'touch of God'? In the previous chapter I considered the nature of the transcendent God who is close to people. How might a person experience this closeness and care? The believer experiences God in his/her deep spiritual self. Psychologists have considered how a person gains access to his/her spiritual self. A person accesses the core of his/her being and experiences God's care by struggling in his/her deep mind, which possesses peace and acceptance, no matter what his/her circumstances. A pastoral care-giver, through pastoral relatedness, might enable a person to reach and be in his/her deep mind and experience God's care. In this way the pastor communicates God's care to those who suffer.

I situate pastoral relatedness within the bio-psycho-social-spiritual model of person and focus on a pastoral care response to spiritual pain. Pastoral relatedness is a key that enables a person access his/her spiritual self and experience God's care.

The Bio-Psycho-Social-Spiritual Model of Person

George L. Engel proposes the biopsychosocial model of person.[1] This model views the person as having physical, psychological, and social components, all intimately connected and interwoven. The intimate interweaving of the different components conveys the reality that the whole person is greater than the sum of the parts.

Michael Kearney advances Engel's model to a bio-psycho-social-spiritual model of person.[2] The bio-psycho-social-spiritual model of person views a person as a physical, psychological, social, and spiritual unity, in which all aspects are intimately interweaving, interconnecting, and inseparable. If a person suffers a serious physical disease for example a heart attack, this may affect the person psychologically in frustration and in anxiety and uncertainty about the future. It may affect the person socially in that the person will not relate socially as s/he would if s/he were healthy. The person's communication and participation with family, friends, and colleagues cannot be the same. It may affect the person spiritually in causing the person to struggle with such questions as 'what is the meaning of this?' 'why me?' The person may be agitated and restless deep within him or herself. Some of the spiritual struggle may be expressed religiously, 'is God punishing me?' 'what kind of God is this?'

Spiritual pain, then, concerns pain at the level of the spirit.

It concerns a disconnection from our deepest core or self. It is experienced in agitation, lack of meaning, despair, torment, a questioning of love, of trust, of self-esteem, of self, and of others.

Acceptance of the bio-psycho-social-spiritual model of person facilitates a more person-centered clinical practice. This attitude puts the focus on the person suffering from a disease, rather than on the disease in a person's body. It focuses on an integrative model of person rather than on the body-mind dualistic model. It focuses on collaboration, rather than on isolation; on holistic care rather than on cure only. It focuses on 'being with' and 'doing for,' rather than on just 'doing for.' It is within this model that I situate pastoral care.

Ralph E. Peterson points to the Scriptural basis for this model of person.[3] Health in Scripture means physical, psychological, emotional, spiritual, and social wholeness. St. Paul prays for the Thessalonians, "May God make you holy in every part, and keep you sound in spirit, soul, and body" (I Thess.5: 23 NAB). And in his letter to the Ephesians, he writes, "In Christ the whole building is bonded together and grows into a holy temple in the Lord" (Eph. 2: 21 NAB).

Kearney maintains that what qualifies a person to accompany another in spiritual pain is the commitment to the person's own inner journey into and within the person's deep mind. It is not so much 'my skills' but 'who I am.' The care-giver must be familiar with the depth journey in his/her own experience. If the care-giver has not made the personal inner journey the patient will sense this. The reader will note that this parallels the contentions of those pastoral theologians who emphasize the centrality of the person of the pastor.

Spiritual Pain

In the context of the bio-psycho-social-spiritual model of person, I now narrow the focus to the spiritual aspect. In an attempt to offer a theory of how a chaplain helps communicate God's care to those who suffer, how s/he might help affect this experience for a person, I draw from Kearney's work, particularly as described in his book *Mortally Wounded: Stories of Soul Pain, Death and Healing.*

To understand the concepts, it is necessary to know how Kearney pictures the mind. He pictures it in two levels, surface level and deep level.

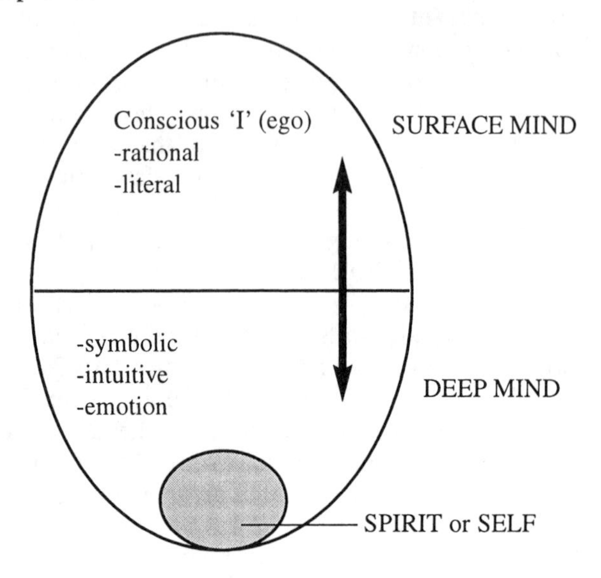

Figure 4.1. The Surface and Deep Mind (Psychological Model). Reprinted, by permission, from Kearney, *Mortally Wounded: Stories of Soul Pain, Death, and Healing,* 55.

The surface mind is the place of consciousness, reason, and ideas. The deep mind, the deep center of which is the spirit or self or core of our person or being, is the place of intuition and emotion, love, trust, desire, the deeper aspects of personal experience. The conscious 'ego' or 'I' likes to live in the surface mind, which is rational and can be controlled, where things are predictable and safe. This is our normal working and conscious state. The ego generally ignores the deep mind of the emotional and spiritual, which speaks through images, symbols, and metaphors. Intuition, emotions, and unpredictability, which are mistrusted by the ego, are buried there. The deep mind or basement also contains old hurts, pains, and fears that have been buried, and which the conscious 'ego' or 'I' does not want to access. But also buried there are deep treasures that enable reflection on deep spiritual issues and questions that confront us. The deep center or spirit contains the real treasures. When a person is confronted with a difficulty, such as serious or terminal illness or some deep suffering, the ego in the rational mind is unable to make sense or meaning of it. Yet it naturally resists the journey to the unknown of the deep mind and spirit. At this time, the ego is in the surface mind when it needs to be in the deep mind, where it can access the deep treasures and find meaning. This disconnection between the surface mind and deep mind is experienced as 'desperate struggle,' agitation, meaninglessness, helplessness, or lack of equilibrium. This is spiritual pain. The ego is trapped in the surface and cut off from the healing and treasures inherent in the deep mind, in the person's spirit or inner depth. The ego may eventually descend to the depth and touch the spirit. For this to happen, what Kearney calls, 'surface work,' which I will address shortly, must be done.

Kearney lists some of the indications of spiritual pain as follows:

- The patient's vocabulary may contain words such as 'suffering,' 'anguish,' 'torment,' 'helpless,' to describe his/her experience, or the care-giver may recognize that these words describe what the person is experiencing.
- Questions the person is asking or feelings the person is experiencing indicate a sense or experience of meaninglessness. The person may ask 'why' questions indicating search for meaning and express feelings of helplessness, despair, or fear. There is a sense of agitated struggle to find a way out of an awful situation. Placing impossible demands on the care-giver to do something may indicate this. This leads on to the next indication, namely,
- A feeling of helplessness in the care-giver, as being confronted with an insoluble problem.
- A religious person may express spiritual pain in a religious way for example, a person may experience guilt about adherence to religious rules.
- Physical pain may not respond to usually successful forms of treatment.
- Psychologically, spiritual pain may be expressed in denial.

- The intuition of the care-giver may indicate spiritual pain in the patient.

Dr. Kearney believes that depth work occurs spontaneously if surface work (explained below) is accomplished. However, help is sometimes needed to enable the ego to reach the deep mind. This help may come from guided imagery, which Kearney practices, or in other ways.[4] I believe that quality pastoral care and pastoral counseling, the essence of which is pastoral relatedness is one of the other ways. Here theology and psychology meet in that psychology, in its analysis of the skills of surface work, explains how pastoral relatedness is created. A person can go on resisting, afraid, and trapped or can tap the treasures of meaning and inner peace. When inner peace is found, the meaning transcends the illness.

'Surface work,' according to Kearney, includes caring for the other in various ways, physically, psychologically, socially, and spiritually. This includes quality time and quality presence with the other. Quality time and presence includes listening empathetically, accompanying the person in a way that the person feels and experiences that the care-giver is really present and 'with' him/her. The care-giver conveys his/her genuine caring attitude, which seeks the best interest of the other. Quality time and presence may offer support and safety so that the ego has courage to descend to the deep mind. When the ego chooses to descend into the deep mind and spirit, it lives with the fear and unknown of this space. In living and struggling with this fear and unknown, the resources of the spirit are eventually accessed. The healing inherent in the spirit can then be utilized and lead to inner peace. In the experience of connection and harmony the ego moves from surface mind to deep mind, and from deep mind to surface mind.

William E. Hulme describes the spirit as the real self.[5] This is where intimate relationship with God, and God's unconditional love, revealed in Christ through the Holy Spirit, is experienced. When a person accepts this, s/he reaches a new level of growth, a resurrection to new life. The real self is confronted and spiritual healing happens.

Pastoral Care Response to Spiritual Pain

Care is the attitude and action that seeks the best interest of the other person. It is a quality that is felt, sensed, and experienced by the other. A patient, a thirty-year-old contractor with diabetes, speaking of Dr. Samuels in Arthur Kleinmann's book, *The Illness Narratives*, sums it up:

> You mean Doc Samuels? What makes him so darn good? I don't know, but they ought to patent it. He is the genuine article. He listens. Doc Samuels know what you're going through. I don't know, it feels like - well, you know, like he's there with you, right with you while you go through a bad spell, an emergency. He wants you to get better. Sometimes I think I feel like he needs you to get better.[6]

Or the experience of another patient, a working class woman with cancer: "Dr. Samuels cares what is happening to ya."[7]

The reader will recall that the word 'care' is from the Gothic word 'kara' and means 'to lament with,' to 'journey with,' to accompany, to 'be with.' The Gaelic word 'cara' (there is no 'k' in Gaelic) means friend, a person who is with the other at the level of spirit. The pastor's inspiration and motivation to care is inspired by and has meaning in the pastor's relationship with God, which is based on the spiritual value of love.

Pastoral care is 'being with' the other, as a person who cares. It supports and cares for the other as that person (ego) struggles in the surface mind in the search for meaning and peace. This care helps the person accomplish the surface work necessary to enable the person's ego to make the journey to the deep mind. The pastor in his/her caring will continue to accompany and journey with the person in the struggle to and within the deep mind, where the person can access his/her spirit and find peace in spiritual qualities such as love, trust, truth, and self-esteem.

The care of the pastor will convey a sense of 'being held spiritually' to the other, as the pastor accompanies the other through pain and search for meaning and peace, the search for which transcends the pain. Robert Frost said, "The best way round is always through."

The key to accessing the deep spiritual self is in the experience of pastoral relatedness where the person can withstand the pain and struggle because of the experience of being held spiritually. David Finlay, an English psychotherapist believes that "the degree to which I can withstand the pain (of being in the wound) is directly related to the degree to which I can experience healing."[8] Very often the pastor will be wrestling with the same question as the patient, yet knowing that s/he has to stay and be with the person in the quest. The pastor spends time with the person, listening intently, getting to know the person's pain and accurately naming it. The pastor lives the question 'with' the person, rather than tries to solve the problem. Oftentimes, there is no solution. When there is a solution, the pastor tries to help the person find the solution that is right for him/her.

Quality time and quality presence provide the person with space in which s/he can live his/her experience and struggle and wrestle with questions, without fear of abandonment. In being heard and accompanied throughout the journey in the surface mind and in the depth mind, the person seeking help can touch his/her deeper spiritual self and experience peace. Having made his/her own inner journey enables the pastor to 'be with' the other in his or her spiritual pain.

For the pastor, the spirit in the deep mind is the Spirit of God. From the pastor's perspective, the pastor 'being with' the person represents God with the person. God is in the pastoral relatedness. The pastor's caring reflects God's care for God's people.[9] This experience enables a high level of patient satisfaction.

Notes:

1. George L. Engel, "The Clinical Application of the Biopsychosocial Model," *The American Journal of Psychiatry* 137 no. 5 (1980): 535-43.

2. Michael Kearney, *Mortally Wounded: Stories of Soul Pain, Death and Healing*, (Dublin: Marino, 1996). Several authors on Religion and Mental Health agree on the importance of working with a holistic model of person. Among them are Martin E. Marty, Douglass Lewis, Vincent V. Herr, William J. Devlin and Frank J. Kobler, Harold G. Koenig, William M. Stanley, Robert Curtis Weikard, Dana E. King, and Bruce Bushwick. These authors agree that mental health is a state of well-being in which the person is able to relate satisfactorily with others, as is appropriate to the relationship. A mentally well

person is able to work satisfactorily.

3. Ralph E. Peterson, "The Healing Church and Its Ministry," *Word and World* 2 no.4, (1982): 325.

4. Imagework is a "technique for facilitating the use of the imagination for therapeutic or religious purposes." Thomas A. Droege, 72.

5. William E. Hulme, "New Life through Caring Relationships in the Church," *Word and World* 2 no.4 (1982): 341-2.

6. Arthur Kleinmann, *The Illness Narratives* (New York: Basic Books, 1988), 212.

7. Ibid., 213.

8. Michael Kearney, unpublished workshop material (1990).

9. A study by Franz Schmidt, "Developing and Exploring a Pastoral Care Model in a Rural Hospital" (D. Min. diss., Bethel Theological Seminary, 1992) found conveying God's love and presence, even in suffering, to be the essence of pastoral care.

Part II

Testing the Theory

Chapter 5

Background Studies

Previous research has examined patient and family satisfaction levels with pastoral care in general hospitals. It found a high level of patient satisfaction among patients and families, with ministry to people's private concerns receiving the highest rating. The most significant study has been "Ministry of Hospital Chaplains: Patient Satisfaction" conducted throughout the United States by Larry VandeCreek and Marjorie A. Lyon and published in 1997.[1] This study followed a similar study entitled "Canadian Patients Evaluate their Hospital Chaplain's Ministry," conducted by VandeCreek and Lyon, together with John Devries.[2] Both studies employed a quantitative research methodology. The new research outlined in this book seeks to extend the research into patient satisfaction with pastoral care by using both quantitative and qualitative methods to research patient satisfaction in an acute general and psychiatric hospital in Ireland.

I have argued that pastoral relatedness is a key that enables people to reveal their private concerns and experience God's care in the context of a pastoral relationship. This chapter outlines empirical evidence that supports this theory, and is by way of background to the new research that tests the theory. The two main studies, "Ministry of Hospital Chaplains: Patient Satisfaction"[3] and "Canadian Patients Evaluate their Hospital Chaplain's Ministry,"[4] were preceded by studies that are of lesser direct significance. A detailed search did not yield any study that directly measured patient satisfaction with chaplaincy services in a psychiatric hospital or unit, though there are a small number of related studies.

Two studies published in the nineteen seventies found that social support was helpful in lessening pathology and hastening recovery from disease. S. Cobb and J. Cassell both conducted research.[5] Cobb found that social support was helpful in protecting people from a variety of pathologies from depression to death and that it could accelerate recovery. Cassell found that people with a supportive environment suffered lesser disease and experienced higher longevity than those without such support. In 1973, John L. Florell published his intervention study on the effectiveness of a chaplain working with surgical patients.[6] This study found that those who received the support of a chaplain healed in shorter time and with lesser medication.

Raymond G. Carey studied the hospital chaplaincy services at Lutheran General Hospital, Park Ridge, Illinois, in 1972 and again in 1981.[7] His 1972 results showed that 63 per cent of patients who were visited by a chaplain were very satisfied with the chaplain's ministry. His 1981 results showed that 81 per cent of the patients were satisfied with the chaplain's ministry. Research by Kurt H. Parkum, published in 1985, focused on the level of patient satisfaction with pastoral counseling in selected hospitals in the Eastern United States.[8] Parkum found that 67 per cent of patients experienced pastoral counseling as helpful.

The Canadian Study

This study is more comprehensive than previous studies in that it was a multi-site project. Its purpose was two-fold: first, to identify the content of hospital pastoral care and the patient and family members response to it; and second, to determine the validity and reliability of the Patient Satisfaction Instrument (PSI). The content and evaluation of hospital pastoral care covered six broad areas: the chaplain's supportive ministry; acceptance of the chaplain's ministry; the chaplain's sensitivity to the patient's private concerns; the chaplain's ministry to help the patient cope; the chaplain's formal ministry functions; and the chaplain's ministry that comforts the family. The instrument in my study is a close adaptation of the PSI used in this research. This questionnaire demands a detailed evaluation of the chaplain's work and seeks demographic details.

Fourteen pastoral care departments participated in the study. They ranged from hospitals with one staff chaplain to larger training centers. Five hundred and eight usable responses were returned.

The results showed that nine items were considered important by more than 90 per cent of the patients. Six of these concerned the chaplain's sensitivity to the patients private concerns. The two items with the highest rating were, 'chaplain let me say what was on my mind' and 'chaplain possessed spiritual sensitivity.' Next was 'chaplain seemed to be listening to me.' Next on this sub-scale were, 'chaplain knew what s/he was doing,' 'chaplain spent adequate time with me,' and 'chaplain understood my problems.' The other three responses of the nine showed that the visits contributed to comfort, relaxation, and reassurance.

On the negative side, many patients felt that the chaplain did not help their own clergy-person understand, or help them with guilt. Patients did not appreciate offers of worship services or of religious literature.

In interpreting the results, the authors take into account both the scores and the percentage of respondents for each item. The following is a summary of the results:

> the most helpful aspects of hospital pastoral care include listening to patients with spiritual sensitivity, spending time with them, and projecting a sense of competency. This allows patients to say what is on their minds with the result that they feel better about their problems as well as reassured and relaxed, This makes hospitalization easier for them and helps them feel more hopeful.[9]

Related variables help explain the findings, including the number of visits by the chaplain,[10] the length of the hospitalization, the person's worship attendance pattern when not ill, worship attendance while in hospital, religious heritage and the frequency with which the person received visitors. The most influential of these variables was the number of times the chaplain visited the patient or family. This correlated with how ill the patient considered him or herself to be and how long the patient was in hospital. I wanted to know how important it is that the chaplain visits are by the same chaplain rather than any chaplain. I expected it to be very important. In their discussion of the American study the authors express a similar opinion. My study addressed this question directly.

Though not many attended worship in the hospital, it was important for those who did. This was the second most statistically significant variable. Low attendance is understandable in acute hospitals, as most patients may be too ill to attend. Hospital services broadcast via close circuit television may make a difference. This facility is available to patients who can walk to or be wheeled to the day room in each ward of our hospital and was researched in my study.

The third variable with statistical significance was the frequency with which the patient had visitors. Those who had fewer visitors were more satisfied though this, surprisingly, was found not to be related to a patient's loneliness.

Participants in the research were asked if the pastoral visits were by staff chaplains or by student chaplains. Four of the fourteen departments of pastoral care stated that the pastoral visits reported upon included visits by student chaplains. The scores from these four departments were significantly lower than those from the other departments. This suggests that visits by the student chaplains may have been responsible for the lower scores. However, the authors do not consider this finding to be trustworthy, as there were many visits by staff chaplains and relatively few by student chaplains. They feel that further research is needed for clarification.

In relation to the second purpose of the study, to identify the validity and reliability of the Patient Satisfaction Instrument, the results showed that the PSI is useful in differentiating the quality of pastoral care. The sizable number of items that showed a statistically significant difference in the responses indicates this. The authors encourage individual pastoral care-givers to utilize this instrument to evaluate pastoral care in their departments.

This study demonstrates that many patients are very satisfied with their chaplains' ministry. The most effective hospital ministry combines both quality and quantity. Quantity is an adequate number of sensitive visits. Quality is unhurried, sensitive listening to a person's private concerns.[11]

The limitations of the study were that different departments of pastoral care used different ways of selecting patients for participation in the study. There is no information available on the different response rates in the various hospitals. This limits the extent to which the results can be generalized. There is no information on the diagnoses of the patients. Nor is there any information on the level of training of the chaplains who made the pastoral visits. Nevertheless, this is an important study because of its comprehensive nature, its principal findings, and the value of the information about the content and quality of hospital pastoral care.

The American Study

This is the most comprehensive study to date on patient satisfaction with pastoral care in general hospitals. Its purpose was to measure patient satisfaction with the ministry of hospital chaplains and to determine the characteristics of pastoral care that contribute to better patient outcomes, from the patients' viewpoint.

The results of this study are based on returns from two thousand patients who were discharged from thirty-three hospitals in the United States and Canada. The Canadian data was that of the study just outlined. The methodology was by means of the Patient Satisfaction Instrument (PSI) questionnaire, discussed earlier. The questionnaire described four pastoral themes, the chaplain's supportive ministry (nineteen items), the chaplain's efforts to help the patient cope (eight items), the patient's acceptance of the chaplain's ministry (eight items), and ministry to the patient's private concerns (six items).

The results in relation to satisfaction with the ministry of hospital chaplains showed that patients value the work of hospital chaplains. The significance of this is to firmly establish pastoral care in healthcare. Of the four themes of hospital pastoral care considered, ministry to the patient's private concerns was the most valued. The supportive ministry followed this in rank. Prioritized next was the chaplain's efforts to help the patient cope, followed by acceptance of the chaplain's ministry. These results confirm the results of the research of Canadian patients' evaluation of their hospital chaplains' ministry, concluding that ministry to patients' private concerns is most valued.

Consideration of individual items in the forty-five item questionnaire, with the results of each question marked on a Likert-type scale showed the chaplain's prayer ranking first, followed by the chaplain's spiritual sensitivity and ability to listen to what is on the patient's mind. This ministry is comforting to patients, reminds them of God's care for them and helps them feel better about their problems. These benefits are affected by attendance at worship services and by chaplains spending adequate time with patients, during which they demonstrate competency. These findings are not unlike those of the Canadian study.

As in the Canadian study, some background variables influenced the scores. These were the patient's age, acuity, length of hospital stay, frequency of visitors, number of chaplain visits, attendance at hospital worship, religious preference, and general satisfaction with the hospital experience. The following is an outline of the significance of these variables:

- Patient Age. While older patients agreed that chaplain's visits helped them cope and connected them with others such as family and other staff, they reported less acceptance of the chaplain's ministry, which at times scared them and frustrated them when chaplains visited for too long and tired them. This made them suggest that chaplains demonstrated less understanding and respect. The significance of these results is that chaplains help older patients cope, but that this must be achieved in short visits that conserve the patient's energy.

- Patient Acuity. Chaplains are particularly valuable to those who are most ill.
- Length of Hospital Stay. Patients who stay longer in the hospital hold greater appreciation for the chaplain's ministry. This begs the question as to whether the chaplains' visits contribute to the patient's readiness to go home. This is discussed in a later paragraph.
- Frequency of Visitors. Chaplains should prioritize patients who are isolated from family and friends.
- Number of Chaplain Visits. As in the Canadian study, the number of chaplain visits is most important. Initial visits are very important but satisfaction increases significantly with follow-up pastoral visits. In my consideration of the Canadian study, I raised the question of the importance of continuity with the same chaplain. In this study, the authors suggest that patients evaluate pastoral care more highly when they receive continuing care from the same chaplain.
- Attendance at Hospital Worship. Approximately 11 per cent attended hospital worship. This probably reflects the patient's religiosity and level of acuity. No figures were collected in relation to participating in worship on television.
- Religious Preference. Roman Catholic patients evaluated their pastoral care slightly more positively that Protestant patients. Patients of other religions reported lower scores.
- General Satisfaction with the Hospital Experience. Patients who are more satisfied with their overall hospital experience were more satisfied with the chaplain's ministry. The authors suggest two possible reasons for this finding. First, staff involving chaplains with problem patient situations conveys to the patients the fact that chaplains are part of the broader hospital experience. Second, patients less satisfied with their overall hospital stay and with the chaplain's ministry may be those who "experience repeatedly problematic hospitalizations."

Comparison of these American findings with the Canadian findings shows that, though ministry to the patient's private issues is most valued by both US and Canadian patients, that the Canadian results are significantly higher. The authors speculate on the reasons for this. First, pastoral care in Canada may be higher quality pastoral care. Second, Canadian patients were required to give consent to have questionnaires mailed to them. Those who gave this consent while still in hospital may have been more sympathetic to pastoral care and so scored it more positively. Other possible reasons may be cultural and religious differences or different emphases in chaplaincy training programs.

Two questions in which the Canadian study suggested further research were whether the frequency of community worship attendance could be used to predict response to the ministry of chaplains, and whether visits by staff chaplains differed significantly from those by student chaplains. The results of the American study showed that the frequency of community worship cannot be used to predict response to the hospital chaplain's ministry. They found that whether the staff chaplain or the student chaplain visited was not significant. The authors suggest that staff chaplains may make more patient visits, provide better ministry to staff, and are helpful with institutional problems. I think that these are valid points. Staff chaplains are more likely to make effective visits in shorter time and have a continuing relationship with other staff and with the institution.

'Outcome Research' studies the effect of the healthcare process or an aspect of it on the health and well-being of patients. This study sought to demonstrate, from the patient's viewpoint, how chaplains contribute to outcome. This study identified the characteristics of pastoral care that contributed to outcome as what 'made hospitalization easier,' contribution 'to getting better faster,' and contribution to 'readiness to return home.' The three items correlated highly, with patients seemingly interpreting 'getting better faster' and 'readiness to go home' as quite similar. The results support the argument that pastoral care is an essential service.

Helping patients relax and providing spiritual comfort were the greatest contributions chaplains made to making hospitalization easier. The other relevant factors, in order of importance, were "helping patients face difficult issues, thus overcoming their fears. This pastoral care helps them work with hospital staff and feel better about their problems. It does not make patients too tired . . . . These patients also report that the chaplain seemed to understand them. This pastoral care does not give attention to guilt feelings."[12] It seemed to me that the authors intended the latter point to be viewed in a positive light. The strength of the association between pastoral care and outcome increased with patient age and with repeated visits. The results suggest that pastoral care, which stimulates the patient's hope, is important to outcome.

'Getting better faster' was not strongly correlated with any particular item. The strongest contributors to 'getting better faster' were helping the patient feel more hopeful, helping him/her overcome his/her fears, aiding spiritual growth, and active listening.

In relation to 'readiness to go home,' stimulating hope is the most positive factor. Helping patients adjust to their medical condition follows this. Other factors also contributed: namely, help with loneliness; giving patients strength to go on, even when visits scare them; help to overcome fears and face difficult issues; and helping the patient relax. This pastoral care helps people access their faith and aids spiritual growth. Helping patients feel better about their problems and the chaplain's spiritual sensitivity correlated negatively with patients readiness to go home.

This brings us back to the question posed above, does length of hospital stay contribute to patients' readiness to go home? Those who received most visits were less ready to go home. The authors suggest that when chaplains pay much attention to patients' problems, it does not contribute to readiness to go home. Maybe patients then focus on 'what can be,' and they want to experience more pastoral care. The authors do not suggest that patients who receive most visits might be sicker, which seems to me to be the more likely reason for their lesser readiness to go home.

The authors make another point that is most important in the chaplain's pastoral care, namely that the chaplain should "always be open to the patient's agenda."

In summary, most appreciated pastoral care involves listening to private concerns, and stimulating hope and prayer.

In weighing all of the individual items, patients judged 'spiritual sensitivity' to be most important. Other heavily weighed items suggest that this 'spiritual sensitivity' involves spending adequate time with patients and hearing the patient's issues. The authors' summary is as follows:

> chaplains provide a context to listen to what is on patients' minds, understanding their problems. This, in turn, leads to patients being more relaxed, reassured, feeling better about their problems, more hopeful, and less fearful. From these results, patients conclude that these comforting visits make their hospitalization easier and give them strength to go on. Subsequent items make it clear that these benefits are accrued by reminding patients that God cares for them, by helping them stay in touch with their faith in a way that helps them cope with the hospitalization, and by praying with them. This promotes spiritual growth. During all this, chaplains convey a sense that they know what they are doing.[13]

The limitations of this study include the possibility that some results may have come from biased samples rather than true random samples. However, the authors believe that, having had two thousand responses and found significant differences in only seven of the forty-five items, that the results are generally reliable. Neither is it possible to determine to what extent patient attitudes were influenced by individual biases for or against religion or chaplains. The results suggest that the instrument is reliable and that the data is not unduly biased. I accept this evaluation as it is likely, I think, that opposing biases may cancel each other out.

Studies in Psychiatric Hospitals

The studies that are closest to an assessment of patient satisfaction are those that measure patient attitude toward hospital chaplains. There are three studies from the nineteen sixties and a study conducted in 1972, which was published in 1981.

A study by Malcolm Gynther and J. Obert Kempson, which

was published in 1960, sought to objectively assess the attitudes of mentally ill patients and of the hospital staff towards an expanding chaplaincy service in South Carolina State Hospital.[14] They also sought to discover the functions and activities of chaplains that patients and staff felt were most valuable. This study found that both patients and staff had a positive attitude towards the chaplaincy service and towards its continuing development. They thought that counseling and preaching were what chaplains did best, and that the best way forward was more chaplains to perform these functions. Patients and staff criticized chaplains who acted 'professional' rather than warm and friendly. A study by Ward Knights and David Kramer, published in 1964, showed high ratings for the traditional roles of counseling and administering the sacraments.[15] No limitations are listed in either of these studies. A study by John E. Haag and Linda H. Jackson conducted in "a private midwestern, psychiatric facility" in 1972 found that patients and staff wanted trained chaplains.[16] The latter authors refer to an unpublished 1962 study by Ralph R. Boyer, which showed that chaplains were as much help to 'non-religious' persons as to 'religious persons.' Boyer concluded that the most important aspect of chaplaincy is the pastoral relationship.[17]

Summary

The empirical evidence to date clearly points to the centrality of pastoral relatedness in pastoral care. It suggests that pastoral relatedness, which enables a person's private concerns to be heard, which supports the person, and which helps him/her cope, is critically important to patients' satisfaction with chaplains. This is more clearly established in general hospitals.

Notes:

1. Larry VandeCreek and Marjorie A. Lyon, "Ministry of Hospital Chaplains: Patient Satisfaction," *Journal of Health Care Chaplaincy* 6 no. 2 (1997): 19-61.
2. Larry VandeCreek, Marjorie A. Lyon, and John Devries,"Canadian Hospital Patients Evaluate their Chaplain's Ministry," *Pastoral Sciences* 14 (1995): 133-45.
3. Larry VandeCreek and Marjorie A. Lyon, "Ministry of Hospital Chaplains:

Patient Satisfaction."

4. Larry VandeCreek, Marjorie A. Lyon, and John Devries.

5. S. Cobb,"Social Support as a Moderator of Life Stress," *Psychosomatic Medicine,* 38 (1976), 300-14. J. Cassell, "The Contribution of the Social Environment to Host Resistance," *American Journal of Epidemiology* 104 (1976): 107-23.

6. John L. Florell, "Crisis Intervention in Orthopedic Surgery - Empirical Evidence of the Effectiveness of a Chaplain Working with Surgery Patients." *In Spiritual Needs and Pastoral Services: Readings in Research*, ed. Larry VandeCreek (Decatur, GA: Journal of Pastoral Care Publications, 1995), 23-32. Originally published in *Bulletin of the American Protestant Hospital Association* (1973): 29-36.

7. Raymond G. Carey, "Hospital Chaplains: Who Needs Them? A Study of the Role Expectations and Role Value of the Chaplains at Lutheran General Hospital," (Park Ridge, Illinois: Summary Report, 1972); and Raymond G. Carey, "Change in Perceived Need, Value & Role of Hospital Chaplains," 28-41.

8. Kurt H. Parkum, "The Impact of Chaplaincy Services in Selected Hospitals in the Eastern United States," in "*Spiritual Needs and Pastoral Services: Readings in Research*, 325-33. Originally published in *The Journal of Pastoral Care* 39 no. 3 (1985): 262-9.

9. Larry VandeCreek, Marjorie Lyon, and John Devries, 138.

10. Three previous studies also found that the level of satisfaction with the chaplaincy services was directly correlated with the number of visits. These studies are: Larry VandeCreek, John Thomas, Arne Jessen, James Gibbons, and Stephen Strasser, "Patient and Family Perceptions of Hospital Chaplains," in *Spiritual Needs and Pastoral Services: Readings in Research*, 343-55. Originally published in *Hospital and Health Services Administration* 36 no. 3 (1991): 455-67; VandeCreek and Loren Connell, "Evaluation of the Hospital Chaplain's Pastoral Care: Catholic and Protestant Differences," *The Journal of Pastoral Care* 45 no. 3 (1991): 289-95; and Sarah C. Johnson, and Bernard Spilka, "Coping with Breast Cancer: The Roles of Clergy and Faith," in *Spiritual Needs and Pastoral Services: Readings in Research*, 183-98. Originally published in *Journal of Religion and Health 30* no. 1 (1991): 21-33.

11. The study by Sarah C. Johnson, and Bernard Spilka named in the previous footnote also found that chaplains' visits were most important as experiences of someone caring and understanding. A study by Jacqueline R. Mickley, Karen Seeker, and Anne Belched found that the crucial factor for nurses in deciding to refer to a chaplain was the nurse's perception of the chaplain's sensitivity and expertise. The study was "Spiritual Well-Being, Religiousness and Hope among Women with Breast Cancer," in *Spiritual Needs and Pastoral Services: Readings in Research*, 215-29. Originally published in *IMAGE: Journal of Nursing Scholarship* 24 no. 4 (1992): 267-72.

12. Larry VandeCreek, and Marjorie Lyon, "Ministry of Hospital Chaplains: Patient Satisfaction," 41.

13. Ibid., 61.

14. Malcolm D. Gynther, and J. Obert Kempson, "Attitudes of Mental Patients and Staff toward a Chaplaincy Program," *The Journal of Pastoral Care* 14 no. 4 (1960): 211-7.

15. This language reflects the terminology of the time, speaking of "administering the sacraments." Today we celebrate the sacraments. I believe many people today would object to the term "mental patients," as opposed to persons suffering from mental illness.

16. John E. Haag, and Linda H. Jackson, "The Acceptance of Chaplains in

Mental Hospitals," *The American Benedictine Review* 32 D (1981): 328-35.

17. Ralph E. Boyer, "An Evaluation into the Nature and Use of the Concept of the Healing Team in Fairview Park Hospital," Masters thesis submitted at Oberlin Graduate School of Theology, 1962. A later study by Larry VandeCreek, "Identifying the Spiritually Needy Patient: The Role of Demographics," in *Spiritual Needs and Pastoral Services: Readings in Research*, 171-82, found that 'non-religious' people have greater spiritual needs. This study was conducted in a general hospital and was originally published in *The CareGiver Journal* 8 no. 3 (1991): 38-47.

Chapter 6

New Research - Significance, Limitations and Methodology

To test my theory and to contribute further to the literature and research on pastoral care, I conducted research in the hospital where I was working for twenty-three years namely, Tralee General Hospital, Tralee, Co. Kerry, Ireland. This new research sought to investigate patient satisfaction with pastoral care and pastoral interventions, and to identify the most significant aspects of pastoral care, as experienced by adult in-patients, in this acute general and psychiatric hospital.

I defined pastoral care in the Introduction. Pastoral intervention means to actively form a relationship intended to be helpful by providing pastoral care. This pastoral relationship intentionally makes one person's needs primary and disclosure is generally one-way. This is an expression of care and concern in the name of Our Lord Jesus Christ and of the Christian community. It also celebrates on occasions the call for celebration of Christian joy. E. N. Jackson notes the tradition that the pastor's relationship is considered to be so close that it is accepted that the pastor may take initiative in pastoral visitation.[1] 'Satisfaction' is defined as "the quality or state of being satisfied."[2] In this study patient satisfaction is measured quantitatively by means of a questionnaire, which includes four sub-scales. These sub-scales measure Acceptance of the Chaplain's Ministry, The Chaplain's Supportive Ministry, The Chaplain's Ministry to Help the Patient Cope, and The Chaplain's Ministry to the Patient's Private Concerns.[3] The quantitative data is supplemented by qualitative interviews.

This research sought to test the following hypotheses:

1. There will be a high level of patient satisfaction among a random sample of patients.
2. Among the four aspects of pastoral care that will be measured namely, Acceptance of the Chaplain's Ministry, The Chaplain's Supportive Ministry, The Chaplain's Ministry to Help the Patient Cope, and The Chaplain's Ministry to the Patient's Private Concerns, the correlation between overall patient satisfaction and the chaplain's ministry to the patient's private concerns will be most significant.
3. The person of the pastor will be an important factor in enabling patients to accept ministry to their private concerns.

This research is in line with the nature of Don S. Browning's Strategic Practical Theology, which derives theory from the pastoral practice.[4] In its application to ministry, Browning's strategic practical theology begins with the current practice of ministry. It then develops a theory from practical experience. The new theory leads to new practice, from which further theory is developed. The process continues in cyclical fashion.

This research is practice-centered in that it emerges from my pastoral practice and experience as pastoral care-giver and Supervisor of Clinical Pastoral Education[5] in an acute general and psychiatric hospital. It was anticipated that current theory on patient satisfaction with pastoral care, and on what the most significant aspects of pastoral care are, would be strengthened, or that contributions to new theory would emerge from the research. This in turn may lead to new aspects of practice.

The theory outlined in Part I states that pastoral relatedness is the essence of pastoral care, and is the basis of patient satisfaction with quality pastoral care. This contributes a theoretical foundation for patient satisfaction to the literature on pastoral care. The new research outlined in this book is conducted with a broader methodology, in a new country, and is inclusive of patients in an acute psychiatric unit. The methodology supplements the quantitative data with qualitative interviews. The research is conducted in Ireland, where patient satisfaction with pastoral care has not previously been studied. Including research with adult in-patients in an acute psychiatric unit extends the sample.[6] As well as adding to building the discipline of pastoral care, it is hoped that this study might aid pastoral care departments argue for their share of limited resources in competition with other healthcare services.

This new research is based on the theory that pastoral relatedness, which communicates God's care to those who suffer, enables people to share their private concerns and have them heard. The nature of God is that God cares for each person.

Larry VandeCreek in the Preface to *Spiritual Needs and Pastoral Services: Readings in Research*, writes that "the basic fact...with which the field of pastoral care must contend is that it does not possess a bank of quantitative research which informs its work nor research programs which produce them."[7] VandeCreek, together with Arne Jesson, John Thomas, James Gibbons, and Stephen Strasser in "Patient and Family Perceptions of Hospital Chaplains"[8] recommend survey research supplemented by interviews.

A research study by John Gartner, David B. Larson, and Carole D. Vacher-Mayberry, published in 1990, showed that research in pastoral counseling journals was inferior in both quantity and quality to that found in similar journals in psychiatry, gerontology, and nursing.[9] The research of Gartner and his colleagues relates specifically to pastoral counseling, a specific branch of pastoral care. However, I cannot find any evidence to suggest the results would be different in the broader field of pastoral care.

The comments of VandeCreek et al. and Gartner and his colleagues refer to research in the United States. If there is a dearth of research into pastoral care in the United States, the country that is to the forefront in all aspects of pastoral care and pastoral counseling in the world, then the paucity of research in Ireland is more severe. Modern pastoral care is a relatively recent development in Irish hospitals. A brief outline of its development to date was outlined in Chapter 1.

Previous research in psychiatric hospitals measured patient attitudes towards hospital chaplains. This research adds to this by directly measuring patient satisfaction with pastoral care and pastoral interventions in an acute psychiatric unit, a dimension not previously measured.

Elisabeth McSherry and William A. Nelson note that experience in the United States emphasizes the need for accountability in departments of pastoral care, as in other departments in the hospital.[10] This is necessary in order to argue for an adequate share of limited resources in competition with other scientifically valued services.

A number of authors note the importance of accountability and encourage pastoral care personnel to engage in quality assurance and continuous quality improvement. Among these authors are Donald Bielby,[11] Lawrence G. Seidl,[12] Mark L. Thornewill,[13] and Earl A. Hackett.[14]

Bielby and Seidl note the need for pastors to be responsible and accountable for service to patients, relatives, and staff in relation to spiritual issues. Pastors need to achieve the delicate balance between objective standards and personal accountability.

Bielby concurs with Robert A. Patterson of the Catholic Health Association of the United States that objective accountability is now essential. It is no longer acceptable, as previously, that quality assurance is accepted on the word of the pastors, out of deference to pastors. Bielby advocates continuing quality improvement in pastoral care. Seidl notes that the rising cost of healthcare challenges pastoral care to show, in concrete terms, that it is a necessary and therapeutically significant service in the care of patients, their families, and of staff. In his experience, chaplains who resisted quality assurance are those who were not involved in continuing education. Thornewill encourages chaplains to engage in quality assurance and to set a standard that can be checked, as a means of obtaining reliable feedback and of showing the involvement of chaplains within the wider caring team. Both Thornewill and Hackett state that quality assurance communicates the importance of the spiritual care of people in a way that is understood by other professionals and by hospital management.

Research is necessary to demonstrate scientifically that pastoral care is an important and therapeutic service to people, as well as being necessary for the development of the discipline of pastoral care. Seidl states that no discipline has ever survived without research. It is essential to have a process, which puts the activities of pastoral care under the microscope. It is important to measure what programs and which chaplains are effective, and which are not.

I hope that this research will heighten knowledge and appreciation of patients' satisfaction with pastoral care during critical times in peoples' lives. And, furthermore, that it will clarify what aspects of pastoral care are most appreciated by adult hospital in-patients in Ireland.

The Setting: Tralee General Hospital

Tralee General Hospital is a 379 bed acute general and psychiatric hospital in southwest Ireland. It provides acute hospital services for a population area of approximately 125,000 people. The hospital provides the following in-patient services: general medicine; general surgery; orthopaedic surgery; ear, nose, and throat surgery; obstetrics; gynecology; pediatrics; neonatology; psychiatry; rehabilitation; gerontology; oncology; radiography; pathology; and renal dialysis. Out-patient services are also provided for in each of these specialties, as well as in ophthalmology, rheumatology, dentistry, dermatology, neurology, and plastic surgery.

The following are the approximate activity statistics of the hospital, per year, at this time: 14,500 admissions to the general wards; 830 admissions to the psychiatric wards; 1,150 births; 40,000 out-patients; 27,300 attendances at Accident and Emergency; 62,300 attendances at X-Ray: 4,400 operations performed in the operating rooms; 1,250 minor operations performed in the Out-patient Department; 1,700 attendances at the Medical Assessment Unit; 3,500 attendances at the Renal Dialysis

Unit. Approximately 402,500 laboratory tests are performed. The Education Center at the hospital is the center for the Pastoral Care training program, and the Nurse Education Program, which includes the Nursing Diploma and Degree programs.

Over nine hundred permanent employees serve the hospital. Approximately one hundred and eighty temporary staff support these at any given time.

The Limitations of the Research

Marilyn T. Oberst encourages interviewing patients and families, either formally or informally, as a good way of measuring pastoral care.[15] Oberst names two studies that found patient and staff perceptions of the quality of care to be quite different.[16] I have noted other studies, which reflect a similar conclusion.[17]

A common complaint about research in patient satisfaction is that ratings are usually high. Differing opinions suggest that this renders the results useless or that most people are satisfied most of the time. It is important to be aware that some participants may incline towards saying what they think is socially desirable or what, in their opinion, they consider we would like to hear. They may feel that, in some way, such responses positively influence the attention they may receive. Or they may fear a negative consequence, if they say otherwise. This study had to counteract the limitation of socially desirable answers. Participants were encouraged by the principal investigator and co-investigators to be honest in their responses. They were assured of confidentiality. The methodology described later will show that this assurance was seen to be delivered. I think it is fair to add that people who are vulnerable and dependent are highly sensitive to listening and kindness, and rate them highly. Many may not know that quality pastoral care-givers are skilled listeners, and not mere religious functionaries.

A further limitation is that this research is conducted in one acute general and psychiatric hospital, namely Tralee General Hospital in Tralee, County Kerry, Ireland. The pastoral care team is two Roman Catholic priests both of whom are certified as Healthcare Chaplains and as CPE Supervisors, a lay woman, who is a Certified Healthcare Chaplain, and Chaplains-in-Training or CPE interns. The interns may be at different stages in their training. This represents a wider range of levels of training than most hospitals in Ireland. Finally, the socioeconomic status of the patients ranges from mainly working class to lower middle class, with few middle class.

The Research Methodology

This research is methodologically multi-modal, employing both quantitative and qualitative components.

The Quantitative Research

Description of Sample

The quantitative research involved the administration of a questionnaire to fifty adult in-patients in Tralee General Hospital. Each of the patients had received at least one pastoral visit. The sample was a true random sample "in which everyone (had) the same chance of being chosen."[18]

The true random sample was chosen as follows: At a definite time, on each of two different days, a random sample of twenty-five patients was chosen. At this specific time a computer list of all in-patients in the hospital was printed in the Department of Pastoral Care. The computer lists patients in each ward according to date and time of admission. The names of the patients in the pediatric ward and the names of the forty-five long-term gerontology patients were taken off the list. Of the remaining patients, all those who were less than seventy-two hours in the hospital were taken off the list. This was to ensure that most patients eligible to be chosen had received at least one pastoral visit.

From the remaining names the sample was chosen. It was estimated that the number of patients eligible to be chosen at any given time would be approximately 180; hence the desirability of choosing two random samples of twenty-five. In a busy acute hospital it is necessary, from a practical point of view, to administer the questionnaire in this way. It benefits the research in that it produces data over a period of time, rather that at just one point in time.

The following method was used to determine the twenty-five patients who were requested to complete the questionnaire. The eligible number of patients was divided by twenty-five. For example, if there were 175 eligible patients, 175 divided by twenty-five is seven. The eligible patients were then numbered, one to seven, on the list. The numbers, one to seven, were written on individual and identical cards, which were put into a box and shuffled. A co-investigator, in the presence of the principal researcher and the other co-investigators, drew one of the cards. The patients corresponding to that number were the chosen twenty-five. A second number was then drawn. This was to have a list of replacements for those who, in the opinion of the head nurse of the ward, were considered too ill to participate, or who did not wish to participate.

Procedure

The principal researcher sought the approval of the hospital ethics committee to conduct this research. When this approval was granted, five volunteer co-investigators, who were not in any way attached to the Department of Pastoral Care of the hospital and who, in the opinion of the principal researcher, were mature, competent, and people of integrity, were chosen. They were instructed in detail about the research, its purpose and procedure.

The principal researcher, or one of the other chaplains, approached each of the relevant head nurses with a letter of approval from the hospital ethics committee and sought the head nurse's opinion about the chosen patients in his/her ward. As anticipated, most of the chosen patients were capable of completing the questionnaire. The principal researcher, or one of the other chaplains in the hospital, then approached each of the chosen patients, explained that a questionnaire was being administered to investigate the level of satisfaction with pastoral care as experienced by adult in-patients in the hospital. S/he explained that those being asked to complete the questionnaire were chosen by random chance and that his/her assistance was requested by way of completing a questionnaire. S/he told the patient that the chaplains hoped to discover what was satisfactory about the pastoral care service and what might be changed and/or added to better meet patients' needs. S/he assured the patient of absolute confidentiality. This confidentiality was delivered by the following method: The completed questionnaire was placed in an unmarked envelope and sealed by or in the presence of the patient. The patient was then invited to place it in a bag, which contained dummies and/or other completed questionnaires. The contents of the bag were shuffled in the presence of the patient.

The patients who agreed to participate in the research were requested to sign an informed consent form. A copy of the signed consent form was given to the patient.

Some time after the signed consent forms were obtained, the co-investigators approached their assigned patients with a view to the completion of the questionnaires. They repeated the purpose of the research and responded to queries about it. The co-investigator assisted patients, who so desired, to complete the questionnaire. They encouraged the patients to be honest about their experience. They again assured them of absolute confidentiality.

Research Instrument

The research instrument was a fifty-eight-item questionnaire in book form.[19] It was adapted from a copyrighted questionnaire by Larry VandeCreek, Robert Brummel and Marjorie Lyon. VandeCreek, Brummel and Lyon copyrighted the questionnaire on behalf of the Ohio State University Medical Center, 410 W. 10th Avenue, Columbus, OH 43210, USA, 1991, revised 1995. The principal researcher received written permission to reproduce the questionnaire. The questionnaire contained thirty-four questions that sought, by means of a Likert scale, to identify how the patient's pastoral needs were met or not met. These questions were arranged in four sub-sections focusing on, Acceptance of the Chaplain's Ministry, The Chaplain's

Supportive Ministry, The Chaplain's Ministry to Help the Patient Cope, and The Chaplain's Ministry to the Patient's Private Concerns. The questions that focused on the first two aspects of pastoral care were phrased negatively and those that focused on the latter two aspects were positively phrased. This, first and foremost, was to lessen any possible positive bias and, second, to encourage careful reading of the questionnaire.

These four sub-sections were followed by two questions, which sought to identify what the patients found most helpful and what they found most unhelpful. A list of suggestions was given with each of these questions. Other questions in this section sought to clarify the important qualities the chaplain possessed and which of these was most important, in the patient's opinion. Further questions sought to identify the chaplain's weakness and whether the patient had a preference for a female chaplain, a male chaplain, or an ordained chaplain. Another question in this section sought to find out if the chaplain who visited the patient was a staff chaplain or a chaplain-in-training. The remaining questions asked the patient's opinion about continuity with the same chaplain; the importance of the pastoral relationship with the chaplain; and for a description of the relationship with the chaplain best known to him/her. Patients were asked to comment on the questions in this section. The remaining questions, except for the final question, sought demographic details from the patient. The final question asked the patient how satisfied s/he was with his/her overall hospital stay.

Larry VandeCreek and Marjorie A. Lyon had tested this questionnaire, known as a Patient Satisfaction Instrument (PSI).[20] In their preliminary test examination of scores from seven groups of returns, they found that this instrument detected differences in the levels of patient satisfaction.[21] A limitation of the test was that it was conducted in one hospital.

The study by VandeCreek, Lyon, and John Devries entitled "Canadian Hospital Patients Evaluate their Chaplain's Ministry," also sought to test the validity and reliability of this instrument in differentiating patient care. The findings demonstrated that the instrument is valid and reliable.[22] This study was conducted in fourteen hospitals.

In 1997, in the *Journal of Healthcare Chaplaincy*, VandeCreek and Lyon again wrote about the Patient Satisfaction Instrument

(PSI). They clarified its two-fold purpose as an instrument enabling chaplains to gather data on patient satisfaction with their ministry at given times, and enabling them to identify the quality and characteristics of the spiritual care they offered.[23]

Among the strengths of this instrument are that it can be used repeatedly, and that its results measure many aspects of ministry. A limitation is its exclusively quantitative nature. In this study, the quantitative data is further informed by qualitative interviews.

Data Analysis

The data was analyzed by the SPSS statistical package. Valid means determined a hierarchy of importance for the different aspects of pastoral care. The data was then correlated to inform the hypotheses.

The Qualitative Research

Why qualitative research?

The principal researcher included qualitative research to supplement the quantitative research.

Description of Sample

The principal researcher conducted interviews with five patients, who were chosen from both the general and psychiatric wards. These people, adult in-patients, were "strategic informants, individuals who (had) been particularly immersed in the experience, yet (were) capable of reflecting and able to articulate that experience – mature, reflective, verbal individuals.[24] They were capable of giving criticism as well as positive feedback. None of the interviewees had received ministry from the interviewer.

Procedure

The qualitative interviews were idiosyncratic and of the conversational type while at the same time focusing on a series of questions that allowed data across interviews to be compared. The advantage of the conversational type interview was that it gave "the participant the support and engagement that the focused interview lacks without imposing the confinement and predefinition of the semi-structured format. It (allowed) the interviewee to share more of his/her own experience or naivete as the two work(ed) together for deeper discovery of the experience."[25]

The principal researcher utilized in-depth interviewing strategies for the qualitative interviews. The questions were formulated from his experience of twenty-two years as a hospital chaplain in seven different hospitals. The latter ten of these years included experience as CPE Supervisor guiding pastoral care interns towards achieving certification as Healthcare Chaplains, as well as being an examiner of candidates from other training centers. The questions covered such areas as a description of the interviewees' illness and hospital experience; a description of how the interviewee experienced pastoral care – was care (God's care) conveyed? if so, how? What pastoral needs were met, and how? Did the patient experience the chaplain as 'being with' him/her? How important was the pastoral relationship and how would the person describe it? How important was continuity with the same chaplain? If the person shared private concerns, what enabled him/her to do this? Was it helpful to do so? How did the person's experience of pastoral care compare with his/her expectations? How important was the sacramental ministry? What was helpful and what was unhelpful? What was experienced as healing about the pastoral care received? How was this experienced? What pastoral needs were met, and how? What was gained that might not have been gained without this service? Any criticisms, comments, suggestions about the pastoral care service, or other issue the interviewee wished to raise. What, in the person's opinion, is the essence of pastoral care?

Data Analysis

The interviews were taped and transcribed. The transcripts of the interviews were carefully read several times and absorbed. The themes that emerged were identified in order of frequency. The principal researcher interpreted the data in the light of his experience as a Hospital Chaplain and Supervisor of Clinical Pastoral Education (CPE), in the light of his experience as interviewer of the patients, and in the light of his theory of pastoral relatedness.

Merging the Results of the Quantitative Research and the Qualitative Research

The qualitative findings were brought into dialogue with the quantitative findings in relation to the four aspects of pastoral care measured namely, Acceptance of the Chaplain's Ministry, The Chaplain's Supportive Ministry, The Chaplain's Ministry to Help the Patient Cope, and The Chaplain's Ministry to the Patient's Private Concerns. Particular attention was given to The Chaplain's Ministry to the Patient's Private Concerns.

The Limitations of the Methodology

Marilyn T. Oberst notes that in questionnaire research factors such as item wording and the location of the testing can make a difference.[26] As seen, previous studies have tested the questionnaire used in this study and found it valid and reliable.

The analysis of the interviews was considered in the light of their idiosyncratic nature. This meant taking into account the personality of the interviewer and how this and his life experience, perspectives, and abilities might have influenced the interview, the thematic interpretations of the interviews, and any other interpretations he might make of the data.

Conducting the interviews in a conversational way required the interviewer to possess skill that enabled the interviewee to articulate his/her meaning of the pastoral care experience in a way that was objective and, at the same time, personal to the interviewee. The principal researcher appeals to his experience. The qualitative aspect of the research was limited by its nature in that the interviewees must be mature, reflective and articulate enough to participate meaningfully in this type of research.

The dearth of previous research in pastoral care generally, and the more marked absence of qualitative research in this area limit the literature and theory on which this research might otherwise be based. The multi-modal methodology of this research contributed towards addressing these limitations.

Other researchers might build on this research by broadening the base to include a number of hospitals. Future researchers might investigate patients' pastoral care needs in particular situations, such as in Accident and Emergency Departments; in crisis situations; with patients who suffer from a particular illness (breast cancer, heart attack, diabetes, or whatever most interests the researcher); or with relatives of dying patients. Future researchers might also research the pastoral care desired in different kinds of hospitals, such as pediatric hospitals, maternity hospitals, community hospitals, and nursing homes. There are numerous possibilities.

Notes:

1. E. N. Jackson, " Calling and Visitation, Pastoral," in *Dictionary of Pastoral Care and Counseling*, ed. R. J. Hunter (Nashville: Abingdon Press, 1990), 115-116.
2. *Mirriam Webster's Collegiate Dictionary*, 10th Edition (1995), s. v. "satisfaction."
3. See Appendix A.
4. Don S. Browning, *A Fundamental Practical Theology: Descriptive and Strategic Proposals* (Minneapolis: Fortress Press, 1991).
5. Clinical Pastoral Education (CPE) is theological education in which the student is supervised in applying academic theology in the encounters of everyday life and ministry. In this task it utilizes the insights of other sciences. It is required training for those who seek to be hospital chaplains.
6. A detailed search has not yielded any study that directly measures patient satisfaction with pastoral care in a psychiatric hospital or unit. By psychiatric unit I mean a unit in a general hospital, which is exclusively for people suffering from mental illness. This is the now the norm for acute psychiatric care in Ireland.
7. Larry VandeCreek, ed. *Spiritual Needs and Pastoral Services: Readings in Research* (Decatur, GA: Journal of Pastoral Care Publications, 1995), x.
8. Ibid., 355.
9. John Gartner, David B. Larson, and Carole D.Vacher-Mayberry, "A Systematic Review of the Quantity and Quality of Empirical Research

Published in Four Pastoral Counseling Journals: 1975-1984," *The Journal of Pastoral Care* 44 no. 2 (1990): 115-29.

[10]Elizabeth McSherry & William A. Nelson, "The DRG Era: A Major Opportunity for Increased Pastoral Care Impact or a Crisis for Survival?" in *Spiritual Needs and Pastoral Services: Readings in Research*, ed. Larry VandeCreek, 309-24 (Decatur, GA: Journal of Pastoral Care Publications, 1995).

[11]Donald Bielby, "Quality Assurance in Pastoral Care in Hospitals," *Pastoral Sciences* 5 (1986): 65-86.

[12]Lawrence G. Seidl, *Quality Assurance & Pastoral Care: Ally or Antagonist – Parts* 1 and 2. 160 min. and 60 min. Decatur, GA: Journal of Pastoral Care Publications, 1992, videocassettes.

[13]Mark L. Thornewill, "Quality Assurance Program for a Department of Pastoral Care," *American Protestant Hospital Association Bulletin* 46 no. 3 (1982): 145.

[14]Earl Hackett, "Quality Assurance: An Asset for Chaplains," *The CareGiver Journal* 6 (1989): 128-41.

[15]Marilyn T. Oberst, "Patients' Perceptions of Care: Measurement of Quality and Satisfaction," *Cancer* 53 no. 9 (1984): 2368.

[16]These are C. S. Houston and W. E. Pasanen, "Patient Perceptions of Hospital Care," *Hospital JAHA* 46 (1972): 70-4; and E. Hefferin, "Health Goal Setting: Patient-Nurse Collaboration at VA Facilities," *Milit Med* 144 (1979): 814-22.

[17]These are Malcolm Gynther, and Obert Kempson, "Attitudes of Patients and Staff Toward A Chaplaincy Program," *The Journal of Pastoral Care* 14 no. 4 (1960): 211-27; Ward Knights, and David Kramer, "Chaplaincy Role-Functions As Seen By Mental Patients And Staff," *The Journal of Pastoral Care* 18 no. 3 (1964): 154-60; Raymond G. Carey, "Hospital Chaplains: Who Needs Them? A Study of the Role Expectations & Role Value of the Chaplains at Lutheran General Hospital (Park Ridge, Illinois Unpublished Report, 1972); and Carey, "Change in Perceived Need, Value & Role of Hospital Chaplains," 28-41.

[18]William R. Myers, *Research in Ministry* (Chicago: Exploration Press, 1993), 57.

[19]Appendix A.

[20]Larry VandeCreek, and Marjorie A. Lyon, "Preliminary Results from a Patient Satisfaction Instrument for Pastoral Care," *The CareGiver Journal* 9 no. 1 (1992): 42-9.

[21]Ibid., 43-4.

[22]The details of this study are related in Chapter 5, 48-51.

[23]Larry VandeCreek and Marjorie A. Lyon, "A Perspective on Patient Satisfaction," *Journal of Health Care Chaplaincy* 6 No. 2 (1997): 5.

[24]Larry VandeCreek, Hilary Bender, and Merle R. Jordan, *Research in Pastoral Care and Counseling: Quantitative and Qualitative Approaches* (Decatur: GA: Journal of Pastoral Care Publications, 1994), 103.

[25]Ibid., 102-3.

[26]Marilyn T. Oberst, "Patient's Perceptions of Care: Measurement of Quality and Satisfaction," *Cancer* 53 no. 9 (1984): 2368.

Chapter 7

The Findings of the Research

The Quantitative Research

The Respondents

The respondents to the quantitative patient satisfaction instrument were fifty adult in-patients in Tralee General Hospital, Tralee, Co. Kerry, Ireland. Thirty-four (68 per cent) were in-patients in the acute general wards of the hospital; sixteen (32 per cent) were in-patients in the acute psychiatric wards. Coincidentally, there was an equal number of women and men overall, and in either category of ward. There was little significant difference between women and men in the findings, either in relation to any of the four sub-scales, or in relation to patients in the general wards or psychiatric wards. The only statistically significant difference was that men were helped more to 'co-operate with doctors and nurses' (r = *.373; n = 30).[1] Women were helped more 'to stay in touch with my faith' (r = *-.369; n = 44). Men's lesser inclination to discuss their faith may stem from a feeling that it is not manly to discuss more private issues.

The patients' ages (n = 48) ranged from twenty-two years to eighty-eight years with a mean age of 57.04 (SD = 18.97). The mean age of the women was 53.79 (SD = 19.29); the mean age of the men was 60.29 (SD = 18.48). In the general wards, the mean age of the patients was 61.00 years (SD = 19.23; n = 32); the mean age of the patients in the psychiatric wards was 49.13 years (SD = 16.24; n = 16).

There was no significant relationship between 'Age' and the sub-scales of 'Acceptance of the Chaplain's Ministry,' 'The Chaplain's Supportive Ministry,' or 'The Chaplain's Ministry to the Patient's Private Concerns.' In relation to 'Age' and 'The Chaplain's Ministry to Help the Patient Cope' the F-score was *2.540. Older patients were helped with coping more so than younger patients. As 'Age' is a ratio variable there is no cut off point.

Older patients received less formal education than younger patients (r = -.617; p < .000; n = 48). As 'Age' and 'Education' are two ratio variables a Pearson correlation showed that overall, through all ages, older people had lesser education. Older patients were helped more to 'cope with loss,' an item belonging to sub-scale C, The Chaplain's Ministry to Help the Patient Cope (r = *.459; n = 20). Older patients also availed more of ministry to private concerns (r = *.324; n =39).

Fifty two per cent of the respondents (n = 26) were married; thirty four per cent (n = 17) were single; 10 per cent (n = 5) were widowed; with 2 per cent (n = 1) in a committed relationship. There was no significant relationship between 'Marital status' and any of the four sub-scales.

Fifty per cent of the respondents (n = 25) finished their formal education at first level; 32 per cent (n = 16) at second level; 10 per cent (n = 5) had a non-degree third level qualification; and 8 per cent (n = 4) held a degree qualification. There was no significant difference between the general patients and the psychiatric patients in relation to education, or between 'Level of Education' and the four sub-scales.

On their own estimation, 12 per cent (n = 6) were extremely ill when admitted to the hospital, and 36 per cent (n = 18) very ill. Thirty-two per cent (n = 16) per cent were somewhat ill; 16 per cent (n = 8) were a little ill; and 2 per cent (n = 1) were not very ill.

There was no significant difference between the general patients and psychiatric patients, or significant relationship between 'Patient Acuity' and the four sub-scales. The vast majority of the patients (90 per cent; n =45) lived within a forty mile radius of the hospital.

Sixty-eight per cent (n = 34) of the respondents received visitors almost daily, while 32 per cent (n = 16) received visitors three or four times a week or less. Patients in the general wards received more visitors than those in the psychiatric wards (F = ***12.089; r = ***.449; Means and SD's: General wards: 1.18[.39]; Psychiatric wards: 1.62[.50]). There were no significant correlations between 'Frequency of Visitors' and any of the four sub-scales. Those who received more visitors experienced the Chaplain's visit(s) as helping them feel more hopeful (r = **.409; n = 42).

Thirty-two per cent (n = 16) of patients were visited by the pastor of their parish. Of those who did not receive a visit from their parish pastor, 40 per cent (n = 20) reported that they would have welcomed such a visit, 28 per cent (n = 14) would not have welcomed such a visit. Thirty-two per cent (n = 16) did not respond to this question. There were no significant correlations.

Sixty-two per cent (n = 31) reported that they attended religious services regularly while not ill; 24 per cent (n = 12) attended occasionally, or only on special days; and 12 per cent (n = 6) not at all. The most recent national surveys that included findings for religious practice in Ireland were conducted in 1997. One was an unpublished study, conducted in July 1997, entitled "Major Religious Confidence Study" conducted by Irish Marketing Surveys for the Council for Research and Development.[2] This study found that 65 per cent of adults attended religious services regularly, 24 per cent attended occasionally or on special occasions, and 9 per cent did not attend at all. The other study entitled "Attitudes towards the Catholic Church" was an MRBI poll conducted for RTE, Dublin.[3] This was conducted from July to September 1997. It found that 65 per cent attended religious services regularly, 17 per cent attended occasionally or on special occasions, and 18 per cent did not attend at all. Thus, the sample of this study is quite representative of the country as a whole in this respect.

Thirty per cent (n = 15) attended Mass while in the hospital. Sixty-eight point five per cent (n = 11) of patients in the psychiatric wards attended, and 11.7 per cent (n = 4) of patients in the general wards attended. The F score was 14.884 (p < .000). Of those who attended Mass in the hospital, six attended in the Chapel; seven participated through the CCTV in the day room of their ward; and two did not indicate where they attended. Those who attended Mass in the hospital were older (r = *.322), experienced the Chaplain's visit(s) as more comforting (r = *-.324), and were less likely to be frustrated by the Chaplain's visit(s) (r = *-.287). Of the ten patients in the psychiatric wards who participated in Mass, six participated in their day room, four attended in the Chapel, and one patient did not indicate where s/he attended. Of the four patients in the general wards who participated in Mass, two participated through the CCTV in the day rooms; one attended in the Chapel, and one patient did not indicate where s/he attended.

The relationship between 'Frequency of Attendance at Religious Services' and 'Acceptance of the Chaplain's Ministry' is statistically significant (F = *3.904). Those who attend more frequently are more open to acceptance of the Chaplain's ministry. There was little or no difference between the general patients (Means and SD's = 1.06[.21] and the psychiatric patients 1.04[.09]) in this regard. Nor is there any significant difference (F = 0.005; p = .945) between those who attend regularly (1.01[.03]; n=31); those who attend occasionally (1.10[.39]; n=12); and those who do not attend at all (1.05[.06]; n=6). Those who do not attend at all and those who attend regularly were more accepting of the Chaplain's ministry than those who attend occasionally. Perhaps those who attend regularly and those who do not attend at all are more convinced about their decisions, while those who attend occasionally may be ambiguous about Church, angry with a Church in which they would like to be able to participate more fully, or guilty as they feel constrained to attend.

In the category of 'Those who Attend Occasionally,' patients in the psychiatric wards were more accepting, though not significantly so, of the Chaplain's ministry. Perhaps illness may have prevented some of those suffering from mental illness from attending other than occasionally, whereas those then suffering an acute physical illness may have made a free decision for occasional attendance.

Seventy per cent (n = 35) were extremely satisfied with their overall hospital stay; 16 per cent (n = 8) were somewhat satisfied; 6 per cent (n = 3) were neutral; four per cent (n = 2) were somewhat dissatisfied; and 2 per cent (n = 1) were extremely dissatisfied. Patients in the general wards were more satisfied with their overall hospital stay (F = *5261; Means and SD: general wards: 1.29(.42); n = 34; psychiatric wards: 1.53(.99) n = 15). This may be because they have shorter stays, have their acute problem attended to, and are discharged more quickly. The Key Activity Statistics for the hospital for 1999 reveal that the average length of stay in the general wards was 5.67 days, while the average length of stay in the psychiatric unit was 21 days.

There were no significant correlations between 'Overall Satisfaction with Hospital Stay' and three of the sub-scales namely, 'Acceptance of the Chaplain's Ministry,' 'The Chaplain's Ministry to Help the Patient Cope,' and 'The Chaplain's Ministry to the Patient's Private Concerns.' Those more satisfied with their overall hospital stay experienced 'The Chaplain's Supportive Ministry' as more helpful than those less satisfied did. The implication of this is that chaplains should attend to the supportive aspects of pastoral care when ministering to those who are less satisfied with their hospital stay. These aspects of ministry are specified in Section B of the patient questionnaire.[4]

Patients who were more satisfied with their overall hospital stay experienced God's care more during their Chaplain's visit[s] (r = .552; p < .000; n =41); were helped more to adjust to (their) medical situation (r = .552; p < .000; n = 39); and were helped feel more relaxed (r = .543; p < .000; n = 46). These patients appreciated the supportive aspects of ministry (r = **.675; n = 15) from a competent chaplain (r = *-.391; n = 44). The chaplains' visit(s) helped these patients with their faith (r = .371; n = 43); helped them overcome their fears (r = .362; n = 36); and helped them face difficult issues connected with their situations (r = *.345; n = 33).

Four patients responded to the invitation to comment, two in the general wards and two in the psychiatric wards. The following were the comments from patients in the general wards: "I am having a good stay here, which I am sure will stand to me when I leave here." And "The kindness and love I have seen from all staff – girls cleaning the floors and everyone. They treat the patients with respect."

In the psychiatric wards a patient who circled 'Extremely dissatisfied' added "lonesome and bored." Another explained why she did not answer this question: "I have been experiencing a range of emotions during my stay and I have been quite volatile. The opinion I give today may change tomorrow, and thus I feel unable to give an honest answer."

Patients Evaluations of Chaplains Ministry

The Satisfaction Scores

The satisfaction scores were analyzed by the SPSS statistical package. Valid means (that is, means for all valid responses) were determined in the following manner: if any one of the constituent variables was missing, the program entered 'system missing' for that variable. The mean of the variable was then substituted for 'System Missing.' This was done at every level of variable and aggregated variable.

The same statistics were determined substituting the 'System Missing' only in the aggregated variables. This involved substituting the mean for missing values that would have been conveyed when the value of any of the component variables was missing. The same means were recorded. For example, in the aggregated variable, 'The Chaplain's Ministry to Help the Patient Cope,' which had the most missing variables, the mean was substituted for 'System Missing' values in each of the component variables. These were then aggregated as before to construct a new variable. The same mean was recorded, while the standard deviation changed from .1296 to .2963.

Because the questions in subsections A and B of the questionnaire were negatively worded, and those in subsections C and D positively worded, it is necessary to have a statistically valid methodology of comparing the subsections. Accordingly, in order to determine which aspects of pastoral care received the most positive evaluation, the consultant statistician recommended that the 'Distance from the Ideal' be taken as the criterion to determine the hierarchy of correlations between patient satisfaction and the sub-scales.

In order to have the results on a 1 – 4 scale corresponding to the scores in the questionnaire, the aggregated means and standard deviations were divided by the number of component variables in the sub-scale. The scores closer to 1 are more positive for the negatively worded items (Sub-scales A and B), and scores closer to 4 are more positive for the positively worded items (Sub-scales C and D).[5] This yielded the findings outlined in Table 7.1.

Table 7.1. Patient Satisfaction and the Four Sub-scales

	Mean	Distance from Ideal	SD	n
Sub-scale A: Acceptance of the Chaplain's Ministry	1.1247	.1247	.3615	50
Sub-scale B: The Chaplain's Supportive Ministry	1.4703	.4703	.4822	50
Sub-scale C: The Chaplain's Ministry to Help the Patient Cope	3.6787	.3213	.2963	50
Sub-scale D: The Chaplain's Ministry to the Patient's Private Concerns	3.8940	.1060	.2508	50

Table 7.1 demonstrates that the findings support the first and second hypotheses. The first hypothesis stated that there would be a high level of patient satisfaction, as represented by each of the four sub-scales, among a random sample of patients. The 'Distance from the Ideal' for the four sub-scales ranges from .1060 to .4703. In comparison with the Canadian and American studies, outlined in Chapter five, which ranged from .22 to .49 and from .29 to .60 respectively this represents a high level of patient satisfaction among the random sample of patients. The American and Canadian studies were conducted in general hospitals. Comparison of the results from this sample of general patients with the American and Canadian results represents an even higher level of patient satisfaction, as the results recorded for the general sample ranged from .0963 to

.3414.[6] Satisfaction with Chaplains was measured on a scale between 1 and 4, so the average evaluation score is 2.5, that is, there are about as many negative evaluations as positive. This represents 1.5 from the Ideal. The results of the study are much better than this. The next section will show that all of the constituent individual variables are also better than the average evaluation score.

The second hypothesis stated that, among the four aspects of pastoral care to be measured namely, 'Acceptance of the Chaplain's Ministry,' 'The Chaplain's Supportive Ministry,' 'The Chaplain's Ministry to Help the Patient Cope,' and 'The Chaplain's Ministry to the Patient's Private Concerns,' that the correlation between overall Patient Satisfaction and the Chaplain's Ministry to the Patient's Private Concerns would be the most significant. 'The Chaplain's Ministry to the Patient's Private Concerns,' with a 'Distance from the Ideal' score of .1060 received the most positive evaluation scores. This compares with scores of .24 and .31 in the Canadian and American studies respectively. This was followed by 'Acceptance of the Chaplain's Ministry.' The next highest score was achieved by 'The Chaplain's Ministry to Help the Patient Cope,' followed by 'The Chaplain's Supportive Ministry.'

Detailed Evaluation of Satisfaction with the Chaplains' Ministry

This section lists the mean scores and standard deviations for the constituent variables ranked in order of 'Distance from the Ideal.' Analysis of these findings focuses on the person of the pastor, the aspects of ministry that the patients experienced as most helpful, and the outcome of that ministry. The person of the pastor and the more helpful aspects of ministry are determined by rankings from sub-scales A and D namely, 'Acceptance of the Chaplain's Ministry' and 'The Chaplain's Ministry to the Patient's Private Concerns.' The outcome of ministry is determined by the rankings from sub-scales B and C namely, 'The Chaplain's Supportive Ministry' and 'The Chaplain's Ministry to Help the Patient Cope.'

Table 7.2. Ranking of Items by Distance from the Ideal on the Likert Scale (n = 50)

Rank	Distance from Ideal (and SD)	Sub-Scale	Item Content
1.	04(.20)	A	The Chaplain's visit(s) were too long
2.	05(.30)	D	The Chaplain was really listening to me
3.	06(.44)	A	I did not feel respected by the Chaplain
4.	09(.35)	D	The Chaplain was a person of spiritual sensitivity
5.	09(.47)	D	The Chaplain knew what s/he was doing
6.	10(.30)	C	The Mass in the Chapel/Day Room helped meet my needs
7.	10(.31)	C	The Chaplain helped me cope with my sense of loss
8.	10(.47)	A	The Chaplain's visit(s) made me tired
9.	12(.41)	B	The Chaplain's visit(s) did not help my loneliness
10.	15(.51)	D	I felt free to share my private concerns with the Chaplain
11.	15(.62)	A	The Chaplain talked too much
12.	16(.52)	D	The Chaplain spent adequate time with me
13.	16(.66)	A	The Chaplain's visit(s) scared me
14.	19(.46)	C	The Chaplain helped me use my faith/beliefs/values to cope with my situation
15.	23(.72)	A	The Chaplain's visit(s) frustrated me
16.	24(.71)	C	My need for the sacraments was fulfilled
17.	25(.69)	B	The Chaplain's visit(s) did not help me stay in touch with my faith[7]
18.	26(.70)	B	The Chaplain's visit(s) did not give me strength to go on
19.	29(.67)	B	The Chaplain's visit(s) did not help me feel more hopeful
20.	31(.75)	B	The Chaplain(s) visit(s) did not help me feel God's care
21.	31(.79)	B	The Chaplain's prayer did not comfort me
22.	36(.86)	C	The Chaplain helped me cope with guilt feelings
23.	40(.77)	C	The Chaplain helped me co-operate with the doctors and nurses
24.	41(.83)	B	The Chaplain's visit(s) did not help me overcome my fears
25.	47(.97)	B	The Chaplain(s) visit(s) did not help me feel more relaxed
26.	48(.88)	C	The Chaplain helped me find meaning in my situation
27.	50(1.05)	B	The Chaplain's visit(s) were not a comfort to me[8]
28.	56(.99)	B	The Chaplain did not help me face difficult issues connected with my situation
29.	58(.93)	B	The Chaplain(s) visit(s) did not help me adjust to the medical situation
30.	61(.97)	B	The Chaplain's visit(s) did not contribute to my getting better faster
31.	64(1.08)	B	The Chaplain's visit(s) did not make my hospitalization easier[9]
32.	68(.98)	B	The Chaplain's visit(s) did not contribute to my readiness to go home
33.	71(1.14)	C	The Chaplain helped me with an ethical problem
34.	74(1.13)	B	After talking with the Chaplain, I did not feel any better about my problem
35.	83(1.13)	C	The Chaplain's visit(s) did not help relieve my worries about my problems[10]

Range: .04 - .83

A respectful (ranked 3), spiritually sensitive (4), competent (5) chaplain offers the most helpful hospital pastoral ministry. This ministry is real listening (2) to a person's private concerns (10). It involves giving adequate quality time (12 and 1). This kind of ministry supports patients in their loneliness (9), helps them cope with their sense of loss (7), and helps them use their faith/beliefs/values to cope with their feelings (14). Further analysis of the outcome of pastoral care, in terms of weighted means rather than simple means, and taking outcome research (which I will address shortly) into consideration, will lead to a more definitive summary statement later.

The Person of the Pastor, The Skills of Ministry, and The Outcome of Pastoral Ministry in respect to the impact of the pastoral role of the Chaplain

In order to determine a hierarchy between the person of the pastor, the skills of ministry, and the outcome of pastoral ministry, I added the ranks given to the three most appreciated aspects of person, the three most appreciated skills of ministry, and the three most experienced outcomes of ministry. The lower score reflects the higher ranking. The results show that, in the overall sample, the 'person of the pastor' (score = 12) ranks highest, followed by the 'skills of ministry' (score = 13), and 'outcome of the ministry' (score = 23). This supports the third hypothesis, that the person of the pastor is an important factor in ministry. This hypothesis is also supported by the patients' response to the question, 'Would you prefer a female chaplain, a male chaplain, or an ordained chaplain?' Though it was not included in the question, 34.9 per cent (n = 15) took initiative to state that it was the person of the pastor that mattered, and not gender or Holy Orders. The findings of the qualitative research, discussed later, will further support this finding.

1. The Person of the Pastor. The patients appreciated respectful, spiritually sensitive, competent chaplains. Analysis of the skills and outcomes that significantly correlate with these qualities enables further appreciation of their importance.

Chaplains who respected patients listened rather than 'talked too much' (r = .948; p < .000; n = 46); helped patients adjust to the medical situation (r = **.422; n = 39); provided comforting visits (r = *.349; n = 46), and helped relieve patients' worries (r = *.337; n = 38). The latter constituent variables are from sub-section B of the questionnaire, 'The Chaplain's Supportive Ministry'. The first variable is from sub-section A, 'Acceptance of the Chaplain's Ministry.' Chaplains who respect patients are accepted for their supportive ministry.

Chaplains who were spiritually sensitive 'really listened' to patients (r = .813; p < .000; n = 43); helped them to use their faith/beliefs/values to cope with their feelings (r = .801; p < .000; n =35) enabled them to be helped by Mass (r = ***.689; n = 21); helped them cope with loss (r = ***.678; n = 19); helped them overcome fears (r = **-.437; n = 35); gave them strength to go on (r = *-.441; n = 39); fulfilled patients' need for the sacraments (r = *.344; n = 36); helped patients adjust to the medical situation (r = *-.335; n = 39); and helped patients access their faith (r = *-.313; n = 41). These constituent variables are from sub-sections B and C, 'The Chaplain's Supportive Ministry' and 'The Chaplain's Ministry to Help the Patient Cope,' with one, the first, from sub-section D, 'The Chaplain's Ministry to the Patient's Private Concerns.' Spiritually sensitive chaplains support patients and help them cope by hearing their private concerns.

Competent chaplains facilitated Ministry to Patients' Private Concerns (r = *.394; n = 41).

2. The Skills of Ministry. The more appreciated skill of ministry was real listening to a person's private concerns during adequate quality time. Analysis of the outcomes that significantly correlate with this skill enables further appreciation of its significance.

Chaplains who 'really listened' and 'heard' patients also helped patients to use their faith/beliefs/values to cope with their feelings (r = .662; p < .000; n = 34); and helped them gain strength to go on (r = ***-.516; n = 42).

Patients who felt free to share their private concerns with the chaplain were also helped: to use their faith/beliefs/values to cope with their feelings (r = .620; p < .000; n = 37); towards readiness to go home (r = **-.503; n = 30); to face difficult situations (r = -*.510; n = 33); and to feel relaxed (r = **-.412; n = 45).

Quality time ('The Chaplain's visit(s) were too long' was the question in the questionnaire) correlated with 'Acceptance of the Chaplain's Ministry' ($r = .812$; $p < .000$; $n = 43$). It enabled 'real listening' ($r = -.698$; $p < .000$; $n = 42$) by a chaplain who was a person of spiritual sensitivity ($r = -.555$; $p < .000$; $n = 45$). Patients were helped to use their faith, beliefs, and values to cope with their feelings (r = *-.424; n = 36).

Adequate time enabled patients to share their private concerns with the Chaplain ($r = .871$; $p < .000$; $n = 44$). Patients were enabled to cope with their sense of loss ($r = .947$; $p < .000$; $n = 18$); helped towards 'readiness to go home' (r = *-.410; n = 29); and their need for the sacraments was fulfilled ($r = .566$; $p < .000$; $n = 36$).

Really listening to patients' private concerns both supports them and helps them cope.

A study of what correlates with the effective use of the more difficult pastoral skills and what correlates with other variables clarifies that the more skilled chaplains enable more positive pastoral care outcomes. The following paragraphs compare the more difficult skill of 'Chaplain helped me find meaning' with the more basic skill of active listening.

Chaplains who enabled patients to find meaning in their situation also helped patients experience other positive outcomes from the pastoral care they received including help with: guilt feelings ($r = .885$; $p < .000$; $n = 24$); facing difficult issues ($r = -.819$; $p < .000$; $n = 29$); to feel God's care ($r = -.699$; $p < .000$; $n = 24$); to overcome fears ($r = -.650$; $p < .000$; $n = 31$); to access faith ($r = -.607$; $p < 000$; $n = 37$); to feel more relaxed ($r = -.565$; $p < .000$; $n = 39$); to be more hopeful (r = ***-.543; n = 35); to experience the chaplain's prayer as comforting ($r = -.495$; $n = 38$); towards recovery (r = **-.508; n = 32); with an ethical problem (r = *.556; n = 14); to adjust to the medical situation (r = *-.388; n = 34); strength to go on (r = *-.369; n = 36).

As already outlined above chaplains who 'really listened' and'heard' patients also helped patients to use their faith/beliefs/ values to cope with their feelings ($r = .662$; $p < .000$; $n =34$); and helped them gain strength to go on ($r = -.698$; $n = 42$).

3. Outcome of the Pastoral Ministry. There was a high percentage of answering for most questions. The percentage of answering of individual questions indicates the elements of pastoral care that were experienced by the patients, and the extent to which they were experienced.

Study of the percentage response rate for each constituent variable (excluding the 'Not Applicable' responses) confirms the findings, as outlined, in regard to the person of the pastor and the skills of his/her ministry, but prompts further analysis of the findings about the outcome of the pastoral ministry.

This analysis considers the items that received a response rate of 90 per cent or more. It is assumed that these are the important aspects of ministry as experienced by the patients. Sub-scale A 'Acceptance of the Chaplain's Ministry,' and Sub-scale D 'Ministry to the Patient's Private Concerns,' are concerned with the person of the pastor and the skills of his/her ministry, while sub-scales B and C, 'The Chaplain's Supportive Ministry' and 'The Chaplain's Ministry to Help the Patient Cope' respectively, concern the outcome of the pastor's ministry. The response rate to Sub-scales A and D is considerably higher than the response rate to Sub-scales B and C. The constituent variables in Sub-scales A and D are relevant to every patient, whereas those in Sub-scales B and C are dependent on the needs of the individual patient.

Comparing the general wards and the psychiatric wards, the percentage response rate is higher for every question, throughout the four sub-scales, from patients in the psychiatric wards. Analysis of variables that received a response from 90 per cent or more of the patients confirms that optimum ministry is that of a respectful, spiritually sensitive, competent chaplain who gives adequate quality time to hear the patient's private concerns.

The two variables that received the highest outcome result when 'Distance from the Ideal' was the criterion were help in loneliness and help in coping with sense of loss. These outcomes were very important for those to whom they applied. They received overall response rates of 68 per cent and 40 per cent respectively. The response rate for both these variables was considerably higher from patients suffering mental illness than from patients in the general wards. Ninety four per cent of mentally ill patients responded to 'The Chaplain's visit(s) did not help my loneliness' compared with 56 per cent of general patients. Sixty three per cent of mentally ill patients responded to the question

Table 7.3. Percentage Response Rate to each Question Excluding Non Applicable Responses

Item Content	Item Percentage		
Sub-scale A: Acceptance of the Chaplain's Ministry	**Overall**	**Gen.**	**Psy.**
The Chaplain's visit(s) made me tired	96%	94%	100%
The Chaplain's visit(s) were too long	96%	97%	94%
The Chaplain's visit(s) scared me	98%	97%	100%
The Chaplain's visit(s) frustrated me	92%	94%	100%
The Chaplain talked too much	96%	94%	100%
I did not feel respected by the Chaplain	94%	97%	88%
Sub-scale B: The Chaplain's Supportive Ministry			
After talking with the Chaplain, I did not feel any better about my problem	84%	79%	94%
The Chaplain's visit(s) did not help relieve my worries about my problem	80%	74%	94%
The Chaplain's visit(s) were not a comfort to me	96%	94%	100%
The Chaplain's visit(s) did not make my hospitalization easier	88%	88%	88%
The Chaplain's visit(s) did not help me adjust to the medical situation	80%	76%	88%
The Chaplain's visit(s) did not help me overcome my fears	74%	71%	81%
The Chaplain's visit(s) did not help my loneliness	68%	56%	94%
The Chaplain's visit(s) did not give me the strength to go on	84%	79%	94%
The Chaplain's visit(s) did not help me feel more relaxed	94%	91%	100%
The Chaplain's visit(s) did not help me feel God's care	84%	79%	94%
The Chaplain's visit(s) did not help me stay in touch with my faith	88%	82%	100%
The Chaplain's visit(s) did not help me feel more hopeful	84%	79%	94%
The Chaplain's visit(s) did not contribute to my getting better faster	78%	71%	88%
The Chaplain's visit(s) did not contribute to my readiness to go home	62%	53%	81%
The Chaplain did not help me face difficult issues connected with my situation	68%	59%	88%
The Chaplain's prayer did not comfort me	90%	85%	100%

Table 7.3. Percentage Response Rate to each Question Excluding Non Applicable Responses

Item Content	Item Percentage		
Sub-scale C: The Chaplain's Ministry to Help the Patient Cope	**Overall**	**Gen.**	**Psy.**
My need for the sacraments was fulfilled	76%	79%	69%
The Mass in the Chapel/Day Room helped meet my needs	42%	32%	63%
The Chaplain helped me use my faith/beliefs/values to cope with my feelings	74%	71%	81%
The Chaplain helped me cope with my sense of loss	40%	29%	63%
The Chaplain helped me with guilt feelings	50%	38%	75%
The Chaplain helped me with an ethical problem	28%	24%	38%
The Chaplain helped me find meaning in my situation	80%	74%	94%
The Chaplain helped me co-operate with the doctors and nurses	60%	56%	69%
Sub-scale D: The Chaplain's Ministry to the Patient's Private Concerns			
The Chaplain was a person of spiritual sensitivity	92%	91%	94%
The Chaplain seemed to know what s/he was doing	90%	85%	100%
The Chaplain spent adequate time with me	90%	85%	100%
The Chaplain was really listening to me	86%	82%	94%
I felt free to share my private concerns with the Chaplain	92%	88%	100%

The Chaplain's visit(s) did not help my loneliness' compared with 56 per cent of general patients. Sixty three per cent of mentally ill patients responded to the question 'The Chaplain helped me cope with my sense of loss' compared with 29 per cent in the general wards.

The religious variables that ranked highly in outcome experience were that chaplains helped patients to use their 'faith, beliefs, and values to cope with (their) feelings,' and that chaplains helped patients 'feel God's care.' The overall response rate to these statements was 74 per cent and 84 per cent respectively. The response rate from patients suffering mental illness (81 per cent and 94 per cent respectively) was higher than from patients in the general hospital (71 per cent and 79 per cent respectively).

There was no statistically significant correlation between 'help with loneliness' and 'coping with sense of loss' ($r = .063$; $p =$

.812; n = 17). Nor was there a statistically significant relationship between 'faith, belief, and values to cope with feelings' and feeling 'God's care' (r = -.178; p = .305; n = 35). However, being helped 'to cope with loss' and helped 'to use faith, beliefs, and values to cope with feelings' were highly correlated (r = .889; p < .000; n = 17). The items that received an overall response rate of over 90 per cent were: 'The Chaplain's visit(s) were not a comfort to me' (94 per cent from general patients and one hundred per cent from patients in the psychiatric wards); 'The Chaplain's visit(s) did not help me feel more relaxed' (91 per cent and one hundred per cent respectively); and 'The Chaplain's prayer did not comfort me' (85 per cent and one hundred per cent respectively).

In order to assess the importance of these outcome variables, weighted means were created. The number of respondents for a variable was multiplied by its mean, producing a product in the range of 1 (the possibility that only one person would use the Likert scale to respond to a variable and score it with '1') and 200 (all fifty respondents scoring a variable with a '4' on the scale). This product was then reduced to a 1 – 10 scale by dividing it by 20, 10 being the most positive for the positively worded variables and 1 being the most positive for the negatively worded items. The use of the 1 – 10 scale distinguishes weighted means from the simple mean scores that use the 1 – 4 scale. These outcome variables shown in Table 7.4 were then ranked in order of 'Distance from the Ideal.'

The three most frequently experienced outcomes of the pastoral ministry were help with loneliness, the experience of God's care, and help towards feeling more relaxed. The comfort of the Chaplain's prayer was the next most frequently experienced outcome.

Merging of Findings on the Outcome of the Pastoral Ministry

Analysis of the weighted means in relation to the outcome of pastoral ministry confirms help with loneliness, experience of God's care, help to use faith/beliefs/values to cope with feelings, and comfort from prayer as significant outcomes of the pastoral

Table 7.4. Weighted Means for Outcome Variables that received a more than 90 per cent Response (n =50)

Item Content	Sub-scale	Weighted Mean	Distance from Ideal
The Chaplain's visit(s) did not help my loneliness	B	1.90	.90
The Chaplain's visit(s) did not help me feel God's care	B	2.76	1.76
The Chaplain's visit(s) did not help me feel more relaxed	B	2.80	1.80
The Chaplain's prayer was not a comfort	B	2.95	1.95
The Chaplain's visit(s) were not a comfort	B	3.60	2.60
The Chaplain helped me use my faith/beliefs/values to cope with my feelings	C	7.05	2.95
The Chaplain helped me cope with my sense of loss	C	3.90	6.10

ministry evaluated. It adds 'help to feel more relaxed' as a significant outcome, and does not rate 'help with sense of loss' as highly. However, as noted, 'help with sense of loss' correlates significantly with 'help with loneliness.' I submit that the findings of this research support including all of the above outcomes of ministry as significant. While each of these six outcomes is highly rated overall, the four outcomes namely, 'help with loneliness' ($F = 1.089$; $p = .304$), 'experience of God's care' ($F =$ **8.924; $p = .005$), 'help to use faith/beliefs/values to cope with (my) feelings' ($F = .115$; $p = 737$), and 'comfort from prayer'($F =$ **6.269; $p = .016$) are the more highly rated in the overall context. 'Help to feel more relaxed' is more significant in the general hospital, while 'help to cope with sense of loss' is more highly rated in the psychiatric unit.

Outcome Research

> Outcome research studies the end results of medical care – the effect of the health care process on the health and well-being of patients . . . . Insurance companies, employers, state and federal governments and consumers are all looking to outcomes research for information that will help them make better decisions about the kind of medical care that is appropriate (and should be reimbursed), for whom, and when. Constraints of money and the

> time it takes to conduct large, long-term clinical trials is a major challenge of outcome research. One strategy of overcoming this barrier is to use . . . simple questionnaires (in which) patients . . . evaluate their own health care.
>
> Foundation for Health Services Research, 1994

The patient satisfaction questionnaire contained three statements that concerned outcome namely, 'The Chaplain's visit(s) did not contribute to my getting better faster,' 'The Chaplain's visit(s) did not make my hospitalization easier,' and 'The Chaplain's visit(s) did not contribute to my readiness to go home.' The following analysis reports constituent variables and background variables that predict responses to these three statements. Table 7.5 gives the 'Distance from the Ideal' for these three statements in this study, in the American study, and in the Canadian study. Each of the statements is excluded from analysis of the other.

The more valid comparison is between the American and Canadian findings and the general patients findings, as the American and Canadian studies researched general hospital patients only. In the overall sample these outcomes were ranked 30, 31, and 32 out of 35 constituent variables. Even so the scores demonstrate that chaplains contribute significantly to outcome. Also and significantly the next section will demonstrate that the outcome variables correlate highly with high ranking variables.

The findings are more positive for general patients than for psychiatric patients. The chaplains' ministry, as it relates to outcome research, is more effective in the general hospital. Nevertheless the results from the sample of psychiatric patients also demonstrate that chaplains make a significant contribution towards outcome in the psychiatric units. The detail of these results is in Chapter 8.

What Aspects of Ministry Contribute Most to Outcome?

The statements that measure outcome are ranked as outlined above. Examination of the significant correlations identifies highly ranked constituent aspects of ministry that contribute to

Table 7.5: Distance from the Ideal of Outcome Research Variables (Overall Sample)

	Distance from Ideal			
	Tralee (Overall Sample)	Tralee (General Sample)	US	Canada
'The Chaplain's visit(s) did not contribute to my getting better faster'	.61	.54	.70	.65
'The Chaplain's visit(s) did not make my hospitalization easier'	.64	.47	.47	.49
'The Chaplain's visit(s) did not contribute to my readiness to go home'	.68	.39	.39	.71

these outcomes because of their significant correlation with the outcome research statements.

The chaplain's contribution to 'getting better faster' is significantly correlated with helping patients cope with loss (Rank = 7; r = -.938; p < .000; n = 18); the Supportive aspects of ministry (**r = .716; n = 15); the patient sharing private concerns with the Chaplain (Rank = 10; r = ***-.525; n = 37); the pastoral relationship with the Chaplain (**r = .481; n = 36); and the chaplain spending adequate time with the patient (Rank = 12; r = **-.445; n = 35).

The Chaplain's contribution to making 'hospitalization easier' correlates with Chaplains who listened, rather than 'talked too much' (Rank = 11; r = **.385; n = 44).

The Chaplain's help in enabling 'readiness to go home' correlates with visit(s) that helped patient cope with loss (Rank = 7; r = -.873; p < .000; n = 16); visits during which private concerns were shared (Rank = 10; r = **-.503; n = 30); and chaplains who spent adequate time with the patient (Rank = 12; r = *-.410; n = 29).

Each of the four aspects of ministry that were researched contributed to each of the three outcomes for patients.

Definitive Summary of the Chaplain and his/her Ministry

A respectful, spiritually sensitive, competent chaplain offers the most helpful hospital pastoral ministry. This ministry is real listening to a person's private concerns. It involves giving adequate quality time. This kind of ministry supports patients and help them cope. It supports patients in their loneliness, helps them feel God's care, helps them use their faith/beliefs/values to cope with their feelings, and enables them to experience comfort from the Chaplain's prayer. It makes their hospitalization easier, helps them get better faster, and contributes to their readiness to go home.

Other Questions:

What was most helpful about the Chaplain's visit? Please comment. (CIRCLE ONE ONLY)

1. **Listening**
2. **Being with me**
3. **Understanding**
4. **Kindness**
5. **Sensitivity**
6. **Prayer**
7. **Sacrament**
8. **Other**

There was a 100 per cent (n = 50) response to this question. Forty-six per cent (n = 23) named 'Listening' as the most helpful aspect of the Chaplain's visit, with 26 per cent (n = 13) appreciating 'Understanding' as the most helpful aspect. Other responses were 'Being with me' and 'Kindness' at 8 per cent each (n = 4), and 'Sensitivity' and 'Prayer' at 6 per cent each (n = 3). No response rated 'Sacrament' or 'Other' as the most helpful aspect of the Chaplain's visit. No comments were offered. In considering these results the influence of the order in which the options are listed and the possibility of this influencing the results must be taken into consideration. However, the aspect that received the highest ranking namely, listening, was also ranked the most appreciated skill of pastoral ministry, as we saw. Consideration of the qualitative research interviews will support the finding that listening and understanding are most appreciated.

What was unhelpful about the Chaplain's visit(s)? Please comment. (CIRCLE ONE ONLY)

1. **Did not listen**
2. **Rushed**
3. **Didn't understand me**
4. **Didn't seem to know what to say or do**
5. **Insensitivity**
6. **Other**
7. **Nothing**

There was a 94 per cent response (n = 47) to this question. Ninety one point five per cent (n = 43) said that nothing was unhelpful. Three patients (6.4 per cent of respondents) said the Chaplain was insensitive and one patient (2.1 per cent of respondents) that the Chaplain was not competent ('did not seem to know what to say or do'). There were no comments.

What important positive qualities did the Chaplain possess?

1. **Trustworthiness**
2. **Good listener**
3. **Kindness**
4. **Prayerfulness**
5. **Warmth**
6. **Compassion**
7. **Judgement free attitude**
8. **Sensitivity**
9. **Genuineness**
10. **Not Applicable**

This question did not yield usable results, as the vast majority of respondents ticked all responses. Participants utilized it to focus on the next question, **Which is the most important quality? Please comment.** Table 7.6 outlines these results. Clearly, again, listening is the most appreciated skill of pastoral ministry.

Table 7.6. Chaplain's Most Important Quality

Quality	Frequency overall (N = 44)	Freq.-Gen. (N = 28)	Freq.-Psy. (N = 16)
Trustworthiness	5 (11.4%)	2 (7.1%)	3 (18.8%)
Good listener	14 (31.8%)	6 (21.4%)	8 (50%)
Kindness	6 (13.6%)	4 (14.3%)	2 (12.5%)
Prayerfulness	6 (13.6%)	5 (17.9%)	1 (6.3%)
Warmth	2 (4.5%)	2 (7.1%)	-
Compassion	2 (4.5%)	2 (7.1%)	-
Judgement free attitude	1 (2.3%)	1 (3.6%)	-
Sensitivity	1 (2.3%)	1 (3.6%)	-
Genuineness	7 (15.9%)	5 (17.9%)	2 (12.5%)
Not Applicable	-	-	-

Other responses were the Chaplain's 'advice,' 'talk,' 'calmness.'

What was the Chaplain's weakness?
Please comment.

1. **Poor listener**
2. **Lack of confidence**
3. **Uncomfortable in his/her role**
4. **Distant**
5. **Judgmental attitude**
6. **Insensitive**
7. **Insincerity**
8. **Other**

Ninety-six per cent (n = 48) responded to this question. Ninety-two per cent replied 'Not Applicable.' One patient (2 per cent) named 'Distant' as the Chaplain's weakness, and one patient (2 per cent) named 'Insensitive' as the Chaplain's weakness.

No generalizations are possible as only two persons gave valid answers to these questions. The patient who experienced the Chaplain as 'Distant' was a patient in one of general wards, and the patient who experienced the Chaplain as 'Insensitive' was a patient in one of the psychiatric wards. No comments were offered in relation to this question.

Would you prefer
(CIRCLE ONE ONLY/Please comment)

1. **Female Chaplain?**
2. **Male Chaplain?**
3. **Ordained Chaplain?**

Eighty six per cent (n = 43) responded to this question. Of these, 39.5 per cent (n = 17) expressed a preference for an ordained chaplain. Eighteen point six per cent (n = 8) would prefer a male chaplain and 7 per cent (n = 3) a female chaplain. The more important finding, in my opinion, was that 34.9 per cent (n = 15) stated that they would not mind whether the chaplain was female or male, despite this option not being part of the question. This entire latter group stated that the person of the pastor was the central factor. There was no statistically significant difference between responses from patients in the general wards and those from patients in the psychiatric wards.

Was Chaplain
(CIRCLE ONE ONLY)

1. **Staff Chaplain?**
2. **Chaplain-in-Training?**
3. **Met both**
4. **Don't know**

Of the 98 per cent who responded 55.1 per cent (n = 27) stated that they met a staff chaplain; 4.1 per cent (n = 2) met a chaplain-in-training; 30.6 per cent (n = 15) met both, and 10.2 per cent (n = 5) did not know if the chaplain they met was a staff chaplain or a chaplain-in-training. There was no statistically significant difference between responses from patients in the general wards and patients in the psychiatric wards.

How important is continuity with the same chaplain? Please comment. (CIRCLE ONE ONLY)

1. **Very important**
2. **Important**
3. **Somewhat important**
4. **Not at all important**

One hundred per cent of patients responded to this question. Forty-four per cent (n = 22) thought that continuity with the same chaplain was very important; 16 per cent (n = 8) thought that it was important; 20 per cent (n = 10) thought that it was somewhat important; and 20 per cent (n = 10) thought that it was not at all important.

The breakdown of the responses between patients in the general wards and patients in the psychiatric wards was as follows:

General wards: 41.2 per cent (n=14) said that it was 'Very Important'; 20.6 per cent (n=7) said 'Important'; 29.4 per cent (n=10) said 'Somewhat Important.' Eight point eight per cent (n=3) said 'Not at all Important.'

Psychiatric wards: 50 per cent (n=8) said 'Very Important'; 6.3 per cent (n=1) said 'Important'; 0% (n=0) said 'Somewhat Important'; and 43.8 per cent (n=7) said 'Not at all Important.'

The noteworthy feature of this comparison is that most patients in the general wards thought that continuity with the same Chaplain was important at some level, whereas patients in the psychiatric wards were almost equally divided between 'Very Important,' and 'Not at all Important' (Chi-square = **12.932; df = 3).

A patient in the psychiatric ward commented: "If a patient meets a Chaplain with whom they are compatible, I feel that continuity with the same Chaplain is important as a bond will form, the Chaplain will learn to recognize the emotional state of the patient and thus their needs throughout their hospital stay."

How would you describe your relationship with the Chaplain whom you know best? Please comment. (CIRCLE ONE ONLY)

1. **Warm**
2. **Somewhat warm**
3. **Somewhat distant**
4. **Distant**

Ninety-six per cent of patients (n = 48) responded to this question. Seventy-five per cent (n = 36) described their relationship with the Chaplain who visited them as warm, while twenty point eight per cent (n = 10) described the relationship as somewhat warm. One patient (2.1 per cent) described the relationship as somewhat distant and one patient (2.1 per cent) described it as distant.

One respondent commented that her warm relationship with the Chaplain "means a lot to me." Another stated that "It's like someone I have known for years – a friend." Both patients who commented were in the general wards.

How important for pastoral care is your pastoral relationship with the Chaplain?

1. **Most important**
2. **Important**
3. **Somewhat important**
4. **Not at all important**

Ninety-eight per cent (n = 49) responded to this question. Fifty-three point one per cent (n = 26) thought that the pastoral relationship was most important for good pastoral care, while 34.7 per cent (n = 17) thought it was important. Six point one per cent (n = 3) thought it to be somewhat important, while a similar number thought that good pastoral care was not at all dependent on the pastoral relationship.

This variable correlated significantly with 'Relationship with Chaplain' (r = **.404; n = 47) and with 'Chaplain's visit(s) did not help recovery' (r = *.346; n = 37). Thus, a good pastoral relationship is a significant aid to recovery. There was no statistically significant difference between the patients in the general wards and the patients in the psychiatric wards.

Comments
'comments you wish to make about your experience with the hospital chaplain.'

Nine patients responded to the invitation to use the space provided at the end of the questionnaire to comment "about your experience with the Hospital Chaplain(s)."

Six patients in the general wards offered the following comments:

(Positive Comments): (i) "Just a few words to say it is very important that, when one feels alone, that there is someone there to listen and not to feel alone. Keep up the good work."

(ii) "Completely satisfied."

(iii) "Got great consolation. He seemed to take away my fear of dying even though it wasn't even discussed."

(iv) "Earlier this year my aunt died in this hospital. She (the Chaplain) was very kind to her and us (nephews) before her death, and also comforted us afterwards."

(Negative Comments): (v) "When talking with a member of the Chaplaincy team, it should be more private. A person would feel more comfortable."

(vi) "I was in hospital a week and a half before any Chaplain came to see me. Patients should be visited on day of admission and before surgery."

Patients in the psychiatric wards offered the following comments:

(Positive Comments): (i) "The Chaplain seemed most competent in his job, knowing from just my mannerisms when saying 'hello' whether I wished to speak with him or not. He was in no way prying or pressurizing. After his visit I felt more content and almost refreshed although I am not a deeply religious person, but I believe I have a strong faith in God and would pray to him regularly – even though it may not be in pre-composed form."

(ii) "Good to help people with guilt feelings. Great presence of God on ward."

(Negative comment): (iii) "Liked if they would talk to me, if they could help me more. I wish they would say a prayer that I would get better."

What Background Variables Significantly Influence the Scores?

Statistical analysis of the relationship between background variables and the four sub-scales extends understanding of the scores. The questionnaire contained thirteen background items. Table 7.7 reports some ANOVA F - scores (the more significant one for each background variable) for the association between the background variables and each sub-scale. Relationships between these background characteristics and the patient satisfaction score now become clearer.

Patient Satisfaction Scores and Patient Age. Patient age is significantly related to sub-scale C, 'The Chaplain's Ministry to Help the Patient Cope' (F = *2.540; p = .035). Older patients cope better with illness. As age is a ratio variable (for which an appropriate statistical test was used) there is no cut off point.

Patient Satisfaction Scores and Frequency of Attendance at Community Religious Services. Patients' frequency of attendance at Community Religious Services is significantly related to sub-scale A, 'Acceptance of the Chaplain's Ministry' (F = *3.904; p = .027). Those who attend community religious services frequently are more accepting of the Chaplain's ministry.

Patient Satisfaction Scores and Satisfaction with Overall Hospital Stay. Patients' satisfaction with their overall hospital stay is related to sub-scale B, 'The Chaplain's Supportive Ministry' (F = *2.602). Those who are more satisfied with their overall hospital stay are more satisfied with their Chaplain's ministry. Perhaps chaplains' supportive ministry helps people towards greater satisfaction with their overall hospital stay.

Table 7.7. The Association between Background Variables and Overall Sub-scale Scores

In each case the F score is given first, with the significance in brackets.
Significance < .05 is flagged with *.

Background Variable	Sub-scales			
	A(Accpt)	**B**(Supp.)	**C**(Cope)	**D**(Priv.)
Patient Age:	ns	ns	*2.540(.035)	ns
Patient Gender:	ns	ns	2.461(.123)	ns
Marital Status:	ns	ns	1.144(.348)	ns
Education:	ns	ns	ns	1.067(.372)
Patient Acuity:	ns	1.641(.181)	ns	ns
Distance from Hospital:	ns	1.643(.206)	ns	ns
Frequency of Visitors:	ns	1.036(.314)	ns	ns
Parish Pastor Visited:	1.387(.245)	ns	ns	ns
Frequency of attendance at Community Religious Services:	*3.904(.027)	ns	ns	ns
Situation at the Moment:	ns	ns	1.144(.348)	ns
Attended Mass in Hospital:	ns	ns	ns	.843(.366)
Overall Satisfaction Level:	ns	*2.602(.049)	ns	ns

The Qualitative Research

The qualitative research consisted of five in-depth interviews. Three of the interviewees, two women and one man, were patients in the general wards, and two, one woman and one man, were patients in the psychiatric wards. All of the patients were Roman Catholics.

The Interviewees

Patient 1. Patient 1 was a married lad, in her early forties suffering from breast cancer for six years. For Patient 1, the essence was pastoral care was "deep understanding," experienced in the context of a "warm and close" pastoral relationship. This enabled and facilitated sharing of her private concerns, which "certainly" was helpful. One of the ways that Patient 1 articulated her understanding was: "They had deep understanding and deep feelings, and they knew what it was like to be in a situation like this."

Patient 1 was helped by her participation in the celebration of the Sacrament of the Sick before her surgery, "it completely calmed me down, and I felt much better going to theatre." Patient 1 felt continuity with the same chaplain to be "very important." Patient 1 related two experiences of pastoral care, received outside the hospital, which were unhelpful. One was the pastor's spiritualizing, theologizing, and sermonizing. "It was hard that I was told I was suffering like the rest of people in the country because I had never done anything out of the way myself, and why should I have to take responsibility for the rest of the people in the country, and why should I have to do it again? This is my second time round having cancer and I have never blackguarded anyone or done anything, never drank or smoked or took drugs and every one else is going on with their lives and doing all the things, and they seem to be flying, and here I am being stuck . . . and anyone I said it (the pastor's approach) to thought it was a bit unfair." Patient 1 also experienced lack of understanding when she experienced a pastor as forceful about her attending a church service for the sick when she was much too ill to go. "I would have loved to have been there . . . . (but) all I wanted to do was lie down." Patient 1 recommended that pastors come closer and sit beside the patient whom they are visiting.

Patient 2. Patient 2 was a married man in his mid-forties who suffered multiple injuries as a result of an accident. For Patient 2, the essence of pastoral care is a pastor who listens and understands him in the context of the pastoral relationship. Patient 2's experience is summed up with the words, "relate," "listen" "understand." It is noteworthy that Patient 2 moved on from talking about "listening" to talking about "understanding," listening seemingly being a prerequisite for understanding. (The pastors' care and God's care) was conveyed to Patient 2 "through their personal and listening capacity. I thought "they were very caring and able to listen and leave me talk away and understand me, you know." Patient 2 emphasized the importance of the person of the pastor, "the approach of N. . . . she understands I think. . . . She was very understanding . . . . I found her fierce understanding." The approach of (the pastor) enabled Patient 2 to share his private concerns, "I think you can relate to them just as good as you can relate . . . to someone close to you . . . I think it was the way she approached me . . . that was most helpful. . . (I gained) "a kind of companionship." In relation to other issues, Patient 2 also felt that continuity with the same chaplain was important. He did not experience anything as unhelpful.

Patient 3. Patient 3 was a married lady in her early fifties suffering from Parkinson's Disease and breast cancer. She was also grieving her Dad, who died the previous year. The essence of pastoral care for Patient 3 is "listening to private concerns or needs at the time" (in the context of) a warm trusting pastoral relationship. "Just to find out what is vulnerable within the person themselves, or within their family and to deal with this." For Patient 3 the chaplain's listening "helped me understand me. . . . People actually listened to what was going on inside in myself." In this way Patient 3 experienced pastoral care as caring and conveying God's care to her. She named the qualities of a pastoral relationship as "trust," ability to "relate," and "relaxed."

Patient 3 was enabled to share her private concerns by "trusting the people that came in." The most helpful aspect was "the relaxed manner in which (the chaplains) came in and sat down." "I think that the people were trained to be relaxed with people who were ill, so I think I trusted that element of it." An outcome of pastoral care for Patient 3 was "by the listening experience you kind of move on a little bit from it. People affect your life and people listening to you affect your life." Patient 3 found it helpful that "he (the chaplain) was comfortable enough not to say anything for a little while, gave me a chance to get myself to think and to look at myself a little bit more. He didn't judge to come in too quickly." Patient 3 related better with chaplains who "gave me time to think . . . . I was quite used to a number of female pastoral care people in the other hospital coming in and out to me . . . . so it was different and I think that is what helped me understand me, . . .(he) stood there and listened to me, it was different to women. . . . maybe coming in that little bit faster didn't give me time to think."

Regarding continuity with the same chaplain, Patient 3 liked that there was a pastoral care team. She could choose with whom "to relate to most within that team within a short time," and then continue with that chaplain. She stated that "I think that has also influenced me coming in here, that I knew there was pastoral care here." Patient 3 said that she was helped by each visit and didn't experience anything as "less helpful." Like Patient 1, Patient 3 recommended that "if the pastoral care person sat by the bed maybe once they have introduced themselves, it would be more helpful, rather than standing over the person talking down to them."

Patient 4. Patient 4 was a married lady in her mid-forties, who was a patient in one of the acute psychiatric wards. The essence of pastoral care for Patient 4 was "to listen." It was essential that this listening be in the context of a trusting pastoral relationship. The person of the pastor enables this. "Because I felt they had special relations with God, and I trusted (the Chaplains)." This enabled Patient 4 to share her private concerns with the chaplain. This helped her relax. "The Mass and the listening" helped Patient 4 most. She experienced pastoral care as healing, "somebody cared."

This contrasted with Patient 4's expectation that pastoral care "would be all preaching, the Ten Commandments and telling us what we should do and what we shouldn't do, but instead we got someone to listen." Patient 4 said that the "group meeting (with the Chaplain) was excellent, it gets people together and we talk, and open up, and we can help one another, and people who don't communicate outside in the ward communicate better after the group meetings, and we get to know different things and try and help each other better, I suppose. On one occasion there was a man who had been a very long time in this hospital and the patients knew he was, and he had been keeping himself to himself, so we, the other patients, went out of our way to make friends with him and tried to get him to talk to us. He seems to be more friendly towards us now."

Patient 5. Patient 5 was a married man in his late fifties, who was a patient in one of the acute psychiatric wards. The essence of pastoral care for Patient 5 is that he was 'heard,' that "I was able to talk out my mind to the Chaplain, which was very good, to get so much off your mind." This was enabled by "kindness and understanding," which Patient 5 experienced, "and caring and very relaxed." Patient 5 found it "very helpful" to share private concerns and was enabled to do so by "the attitude and the trust" conveyed by the Chaplain. Patient 5 described the pastoral relationships he experienced as "very warm and helpful." He considers it "very important" to have continuity with the same Chaplain "because you get to know one another better and develop within the relationship." Patient 5 experienced the Chaplain's group as "very good, and it was very interesting I thought, everybody was entitled to give their own opinion in the group and everybody did, which was very nice."

Merging the Findings of the Quantitative Research and the Qualitative Research

The qualitative findings can now be brought into dialogue with the quantitative findings in relation to the four aspects of pastoral care measured namely, Acceptance of the Chaplain's Ministry, The Chaplain's Supportive Ministry, The Chaplain's Ministry to Help the Patient Cope, and The Chaplain's Ministry to the Patient's Private Concerns. Particular attention is given to The Chaplain's Ministry to the Patient's Private Concerns.

The quantitative research found that there was a high level of patient satisfaction with pastoral care among the random sample of patients. And that among the four aspects of pastoral care to be measured the correlation between overall Patient Satisfaction and the Chaplain's Ministry to the Patient's Private Concerns was the most significant. The person of the pastor was found to be an important factor.

A respectful, spiritually sensitive, competent chaplain offers the most helpful hospital pastoral ministry. This ministry is real listening to a person's private concerns. It involves giving adequate quality time. This kind of ministry supports patients in their loneliness, helps them feel God's care, helps them relax more, and helps them experience comfort from the Chaplain's prayer.

The qualitative research supports these findings. The summaries of the interviews reveal a high level of Acceptance of the Chaplain's Ministry. Each of the interviewees experienced 'warm' and 'trusting' pastoral relationships. The person of the pastor (reflected in sub-scales A and D) was found to be the factor that most enabled the Chaplain's Ministry to the Patient's Private Concerns (sub-scale D). The qualitative interviews confirmed that the Chaplain's listening ministry to the patient's private concerns was the most significant aspect of the Chaplain's pastoral ministry. Four of the five interviewees named listening as the essence of pastoral care, and Patient 1 named 'deep understanding.' We saw that listening is a prerequisite for understanding. Each of the five interviewees shared their private concerns with the Chaplain. "Deep understanding," experienced in the context of a "warm and close" pastoral relationship, enabled Patient 1 to share her private concerns with the chaplain and this "certainly" was helpful. The "relational" approach of the Chaplain enabled Patient 2 to share his private concerns. "Trust," "ability to relate," and "ability to be relaxed" enabled Patient 3 to share her "private concerns or needs at the time." "Trust" enabled Patient 4 to share her private concerns. Patient 4's sharing of her private concerns helped her relax more. "Kindness and understanding" enabled Patient 5 to "talk out my mind to the Chaplain," and this got "so much off my mind."

Sub-scales B and C namely, 'The Chaplain's Supportive Ministry,' and 'The Chaplain's Ministry to Help the Patient Cope,' measured the outcome of the pastoral ministry. The quantitative research found that help with loneliness, help in experiencing God's care, help towards feeling more relaxed, and comfort received from the Chaplain's prayer to be the most frequently experienced outcomes of the Chaplain' pastoral ministry. Each of these outcomes is an aspect of the Chaplain's supportive ministry. The qualitative research reveals high support for the finding that the chaplain's supportive ministry helps patients experience God's care. Patients 2, 3, and 4 confirmed this. Patient 3 and Patient 4 were helped to relax more. The relaxed nature of the pastoral relationship enabled Patient 3 to relax more, while Patient 4 was enabled to do so by sharing her private concerns. The availability of pastoral care in this hospital influenced Patient 3 in her choice of hospital. Patient 1 experienced the support of the Chaplain's prayer and of the Sacrament of the Sick.

Sub-scale C, 'The Chaplain's Ministry to Help the Patient Cope,' requires a higher level of skill from the Chaplain. The

Chaplain's listening helped Patient 3 to gain insight and find meaning, "helped me understand me . . . (and) move on a little bit from it."

The qualitative research confirmed the recommendation of a patient who commented in the questionnaire that chaplains should create more privacy when talking with a patient. Both Patient 1 and Patient 3 recommended that the chaplain sit by the patient whom s/he is visiting.

Conclusion

This research supports the theory that pastoral relatedness, as it is defined in Chapter 1, is the essence of pastoral care. A respectful, spiritually sensitive, and competent chaplain best conveys pastoral relatedness in the context of a loving, trusting, warm, and understanding pastoral relationship.

The findings of this research have implications for those who interview candidates seeking degrees in Healthcare Chaplaincy or Certification as Healthcare Chaplains, and for those who interview applicants for Hospital Chaplaincy posts. These findings support the current practice of making decisions about candidates for Certification based on the personal competence, theological competence, and professional competence, and the integration of these competencies. Those who interview applicants for Hospital Chaplaincy posts should be keenly aware of the importance of the person of the pastor whom they recommend for the post, as well as of his/her competencies.

An interesting finding in relation to patients in the psychiatric unit was that continuity with the same Chaplain was not important to a significant minority of patients in the psychiatric unit. This may point to the importance of the symbolic meaning of chaplain for some patients suffering mental illness.

The impact and value of the Chaplain's weekly group with patients from the psychiatric wards was much more powerful than I anticipated. This was a significant finding of the qualitative interviews and would not have been discovered by the questionnaire alone.

This research also supports the value of CCTV from the Chapel to the hospital wards day rooms. Of those who participated in

Mass in the hospital, half participated through the CCTV in the day rooms. Presumably these patients would have been unable to participate were it not for the availability of the hospital Mass on CCTV. The opportunity to participate in Mass was particularly important to patients in the psychiatric wards, as was confirmed in the qualitative interviews with the patients from those wards.

While most chaplains are aware of the changing nature of hospital ministry, with the emphasis on relatedness replacing the more functional ministry, this changing emphasis is expressed more forcibly than might have been expected in the finding that no patient experienced 'sacrament' as the most helpful aspect of pastoral ministry. In Chapter 2, I outlined the changing emphases in pastoral care over the centuries. The nature and essence of Jesus' pastoral care, and the pastoral care of the early Church, was a trusting relationship, based on the relationship between the Father and Son. During the third century the emphasis changed, and from then until the twentieth century, the necessity of the sacraments was strongly emphasized. The twentieth century reflected the transition towards the primacy of pastoral relationship again. This research found that this continuing development has advanced further than some pastors might realize. Planners of hospital chaplaincy services will be aware of lesser need of ordained chaplains in terms of pastoral ministry, though the constant availability of ordained minister continues to be a serious expectation, especially of relatives of seriously ill patients.

The findings of this research reveal that hospital chaplains are highly valued for the persons that they are, the skills that they possess, and for the outcome of their pastoral ministry.

Notes:

1. * $p = < .05$; ** $p = < .01$; ***$p < .001$. When $p < .000$ this is stated.
2. Ann Hanley, "Major Religious Confidence Study," Intercom, (March 1998): 18-9.
3. RTE is the national broadcasting station encompassing both radio and television.
4. See Table 7.3 in this Chapter or Appendix A.
5. This research found that it was not significant whether the questions were phrased positively or negatively.
6. See Table 8.1 on p. 113.
7. Crosstabs revealed that patients in the psychiatric wards were helped more to stay

in touch with their faith. Gen.: 0% strongly agreed. Psy.: 12.5% strongly agreed.

8. Crosstabs revealed differences at either end of the scale between general patients and psychiatric patients. Gen.: 87.5% strongly disagreed; 3.1% mildly disagreed; 3.1% mildly agreed; and 6.3% strongly agreed. Psy.: 62.5% strongly disagreed; 6.3% mildly disagreed; 6.3% mildly agreed; and 25% strongly agreed.

9. Crosstabs revealed that chaplains were more successful at making hospitalization easier for general patients than for psychiatric patients. Gen.: 70% strongly disagreed; 20% mildly disagreed; 3.3% mildly agreed; and 6.7% strongly agreed. Psy.: 64.3% strongly disagreed; 0% mildly disagreed; 7.1% mildly agreed; and 28.6% strongly agreed. The bigger differences are with those who strongly agreed.

10. Crosstabs revealed that worries were relieved more for patients in the general wards. Gen.: 60% of respondents strongly disagreed; 24%mildly disagreed; 8% mildly agreed; and 8% strongly agreed.

Chapter 8

Separate Analyses of the General Wards and the Psychiatric Wards

The same analyses, which were applied to the overall sample, were applied separately to the general wards and to the psychiatric wards. Tables 8.1 and 8.2 outline the results.

Table 8.1. Patient Satisfaction and the Four Sub-scales (The General Wards)

	Mean	Distance from Ideal	SD	n
Sub-scale A: Acceptance of the Chaplain's Ministry	1.1188	.1188	.3944	34
Sub-scale B: The Chaplain's Supportive Ministry	1.3414	.3414	.3477	34
Sub-scale C: The Chaplain's Ministry to Help the Patient Cope	3.7149	.2851	.2455	34
Sub-scale D: The Chaplain's Ministry to the Patient's Private Concerns	3.9037	.0963	.2123	34

Table 8.1 demonstrates that patients in the general wards scored the four aspects of pastoral ministry in the same order as in the overall sample, but with slightly higher scores. The 'Distance from the Ideal' was less for each sub-scale.

Table 8.2. Patient Satisfaction and the Four Sub-scales (The Psychiatric Wards)

	Mean	Distance from Ideal	SD	n
Sub-scale A: Acceptance of the Chaplain's Ministry	1.1372	.1372	.2901	16
Sub-scale B: The Chaplain's Supportive Ministry	1.7443	.7443	.6131	16
Sub-scale C: The Chaplain's Ministry to Help the Patient Cop	3.6017	.3983	.3806	16
Sub-scale D: The Chaplain's Ministry to the Patient's Private Concerns	3.8733	.1267	.3250	16

Table 8.2 demonstrates that patients in the psychiatric wards also scored the four aspects of ministry in the same order as patients in the overall sample, but with slightly lower scores. The 'Distance from the Ideal' was more for each sub-scale.

Overall, the satisfaction scores were higher from patients in the general wards, the gap being widest for 'The Chaplain's Supportive Ministry,' (F = *7.78, the only significant F score) and narrowest for 'Acceptance of the Chaplain's Ministry.'

Detailed Evaluation of Satisfaction with the Chaplain's Ministry: General Wards and Psychiatric Wards Analyzed Separately

This section lists the mean scores and standard deviations for the constituent variables ranked in order of 'Distance from the Ideal' for the general wards and for the psychiatric wards separately. Analysis of these findings focuses on the person of the pastor, the aspects of ministry that the patients experienced as most helpful, and the outcome of that ministry. The person of the pastor and the more helpful aspects of ministry are determined by rankings from sub-scales A and D namely, 'Acceptance of the Chaplain's Ministry' and 'The Chaplain's Ministry to the Patient's Private Concerns.' The outcome of ministry is determined by the rankings from sub-scales B and C namely, 'The Chaplain's Supportive Ministry' and 'The Chaplain's Ministry to Help the Patient Cope.'

Table 8.3 demonstrates that a competent (ranked 1), respectful (6), spiritually sensitive (12) chaplain offers the most helpful ministry in the acute general hospital. This ministry is real listening (5) and appropriate prayer (9), which enables patients to share their private concerns (11). This involves giving adequate quality time (3 and 7). This ministry supports patients in their loneliness (2), enables them to experience God's care (4), and gives them the strength to go on (10). It helps patients cope with their sense of loss (8).

Table 8.4, Ranking of items by 'Distance from the Ideal' for the Psychiatric wards (n =16) demonstrates that a respectful (ranked 1), spiritually sensitive (2), competent (11) chaplain, offers the most helpful ministry in the acute psychiatric wards. This chaplain offers real listening (5) during adequate quality time (3 and 14). This enables patients to share their private concerns (10). Mass is most important in meeting patients' needs. This ministry supports patients in their loneliness (13), helps patients cope with their sense of loss (7), and helps them utilize their faith, values, and beliefs to cope with their feelings (9).

All patients are consistent in identifying respect, spiritual sensitivity, and competency as the important qualities of the pastor. In relation to ministry, the patients most appreciated quality time spent listening to their private concerns. This helped them in their loneliness, and helped them cope with their sense of loss. Patients in the general wards appreciated private prayer, while patients suffering mental illness appreciated formal worship.

Table 8.3. Ranking of Items by Distance from the Ideal on the Likert Scale for the General Wards (n = 34)

Rank	Distance from Ideal (and SD)	Sub-scale	Item Content
1.	03(.19)	D	The Chaplain knew what s/he was doing
2	.05(.23)	B	The Chaplain's visit(s) did not help my loneliness
3	.06(.24)	A	The Chaplain's visit(s) were too long
4	.07(.27)	B	The Chaplain's visit(s) did not help me feel God's care
5	.07(.38)	D	The Chaplain was really listening to me
6	.09(.52)	A	I did not feel respected by the Chaplain
7	.10(.31)	D	The Chaplain spent adequate time with me
8	.10(.32)	C	The Chaplain helped me cope with my sense of loss
9	.10(.41)	B	The Chaplain's prayer did not comfort me
10	.11(.42)	B	The Chaplain's visit(s) did not give me the strength to go on
11	.13(.35)	D	I felt free to share my private concerns with the Chaplain
12	.13(.43)	D	The Chaplain was a person of spiritual sensitivity
13	.13(.55)	A	The Chaplain's visit(s) made me tired
14	.13(.55)	A	The Chaplain's visit(s) frustrated me
15	.14(.36)	A	The Chaplain's visit(s) did not help me stay in touch with my faith
17	.15(.36)	B	The Chaplain's visit(s) did not help me feel more hopeful
18	.15(.53)	C	My need for the sacraments was fulfilled
19	.15(.38)	C	The Chaplain helped me cope with guilt feelings
20	.18(.40)	C	The Mass in the Chapel/Day Room helped meet my needs
21	.18(.73)	A	The Chaplain's visit(s) scared me
22	.19(.48)	B	The Chaplain's visit(s) did not help me feel more relaxed
23	.21(.51)	C	The Chaplain helped me use my faith/beliefs/values to cope with my feelings
24	.28(.81)	B	The Chaplain's visit(s) did not comfort me
25	.35(.67)	B	The Chaplain did not help me face difficult issues connected with my situation
26	.36(.70)	C	The Chaplain helped me find meaning in my situation
27	.37(.68)	C	The Chaplain helped me co-operate with the doctors and nurses
28	.37(.74)	C	The Chaplain helped me with an ethical problem
29	.38(.82)	B	The Chaplain's visit(s) did not help me overcome my fears
30	.39(.61)	B	The Chaplain's visit(s) did not contribute to my readiness to go home
31	.44(.89)	B	After talking with the Chaplain, I did not feel any better about my problem
32	.47(.86)	B	The Chaplain's visit(s) did not make my hospitalization easier
33	.54(.83)	B	The Chaplain's visit(s) did not contribute to my getting better faster
34	.54(.90)	B	The Chaplain's visit(s) did not help me adjust to the medical situation
35	.64(.95)	B	The Chaplain's visit(s) did not help relieve my worries about my problems

Range: .03 - .64

Table 8.4. Ranking of Items by Distance from the Ideal on the Likert Scale for the Psychiatric Wards (n = 16)

Rank	Distance from Ideal (and SD)	Sub-scale	Item Content
1	.00(.00)	A	I did not feel respected by the Chaplain
2	.00(.00)	D	The Chaplain was a person of spiritual sensitivity
3	.00(.00)	A	The Chaplain's visit(s) were too long
4	.00(.00)	C	The Mass in the Chapel/Day Room helped meet my needs
5	.00(.75)	D	The Chaplain was really listening to me
6	.06(.25)	A	The Chaplain's visit(s) made me tired
7	.10(.32)	C	The Chaplain helped me cope with my sense of loss
8	.13(.50)	A	The Chaplain's visit(s) scared me
9	.15(.38)	C	The Chaplain helped me use my faith/beliefs/values to cope with my feelings
10	.19(.75)	D	I felt free to share my private concerns with the Chaplain
11	.19(.75)	D	The Chaplain knew what s/he was doing
12	.19(.75)	A	The Chaplain talked too much
13	.20(.56)	B	The Chaplain's visit(s) did not help my loneliness
14	.25(.77)	D	The Chaplain spent adequate time with me
15	.44(.96)	A	The Chaplain's visit(s) frustrated me
16	.44(1.03)	B	The Chaplain did not help me stay in touch with my faith
17	.45(.93)	C	The Chaplain helped me co-operate with the doctors and nurses
18	.45(1.04)	C	My need for the sacraments was fulfilled
19	.46(.88)	B	The Chaplain did not help me overcome my fears
20	.53(.99)	B	The Chaplain's visit(s) did not help me feel more hopeful
21	.53(.99)	B	The Chaplain's visit(s) did not give me the strength to go on
22	.58(1.16)	C	The Chaplain helped me cope with guilt feelings
23	.64(1.01)	B	The Chaplain's visit(s) did not help me adjust to the medical situation
24	.67(1.11)	C	The Chaplain helped me find meaning in my situation
25	.69(1.14)	B	The Chaplain's prayer did not comfort me
26	.71(1.20)	B	The Chaplain's visit(s) did not contribute to my getting better faster
27	.73(1.10)	B	The Chaplain's visit(s) did not help me feel God's care
28	.86(1.29)	B	The Chaplain did not help me face difficult issues connected with my situation
29	.94(1.34)	B	The Chaplain's visit(s) were not a comfort to me
30	1.00(1.41)	B	The Chaplain's visit(s) did not make my hospitalization easier
31	1.00(1.41)	B	The Chaplain's visit(s) did not help me feel more relaxed
32	1.08(1.26)	B	The Chaplain's visit(s) did not help my readiness to go home
33	1.13(1.36)	B	The Chaplain's visit(s) did not help relieve my worries about my problems
34	1.17(1.47)	C	The Chaplain helped me with an ethical problem
35	1.27(1.33)	B	After talking with the Chaplain, I did not feel any better about my problem

The Person of the Pastor, The Skills of Ministry, and The Outcome of Pastoral Ministry in respect to the impact of the pastoral role of the Chaplain

In order to determine a hierarchy between the person of the pastor, the skills of ministry, and the outcome of pastoral ministry, I added the ranks given to the three most appreciated aspect of person, the three most appreciated skills of ministry, and the three most experienced outcomes of ministry. The lower score reflects the higher ranking. While there was general agreement on the aspects of person, of skills, and the elements of outcome, patients in the general wards ranked outcome (score =13) highest, with person and skills both scoring nineteen. Patients in the psychiatric unit ranked person (score = 15), ministry (score = 22), and outcome (score =29), in that order. An implication of this is the relative importance of the person of the pastor for ministry to patients suffering mental illness, and for pastors ministering in more general settings, the importance of satisfactory ministry outcomes delivered by a competent pastor utilizing the skills of ministry.

Further Discussion on the Outcome of the Pastoral Ministry

In order to assess the importance of outcome variables, weighted means were created for the general sample and for the psychiatric sample in the same way as for the overall sample.

Table 8.5 demonstrates that the two outcomes most appreciated by the general patients were the same as for the overall sample namely, help with loneliness and help in feeling God's care. The chaplain's prayer was the third most appreciated outcome, with help towards feeling more relaxed fourth.

Table 8.6 demonstrates that the findings in the psychiatric setting were the same as those for the overall sample, help with loneliness, help to feel God's care, and help to feel more relaxed. The Chaplain's prayer was the fourth most appreciated outcome. The only difference between the general patients and the psychiatric patients was the exchange of rankings three and four between 'help to feel more relaxed,' and 'the comfort of the Chaplain's prayer.' 'Help to feel more relaxed' was rated slightly more highly among the general hospital patients, while the psychiatric patients rated 'the comfort of the Chaplain's prayer slightly more highly.

Table 8.5. Weighted Means for Outcome Variables that received a more than 90 per cent Response (General Wards Sample: n = 34)

Item Content	Sub-Scale	Weighted Mean	Distance from Ideal
The Chaplain's visit(s) did not help my loneliness	B	1.00	.00
The Chaplain's visit(s) did not help me feel God's care	B	1.44	.44
The Chaplain's prayer was not a comfort	B	1.60	.60
The Chaplain's visit(s) did not help me feel more relaxed	B	1.84	.84
The Chaplain's visit(s) were not a comfort	B	2.05	1.05
The Chaplain helped me use my faith/beliefs/values to cope with my feelings	B	4.55	5.45
The Chaplain helped me cope with my sense of loss	B	3.90	6.10

Table 8.6. Weighted Means for Outcome Variables that received a more than 90 per cent Response (Psychiatric Wards Sample: n = 16)

Item Content	Sub-scale	Weighted Mean	Distance from Ideal
The Chaplain's visit(s) did not help my loneliness	B	0.90	-.10
The Chaplain's visit(s) did not help me feel God's care	B	1.30	.30
The Chaplain's visit(s) did not help me feel more relaxed	B	1.60	.60
The Chaplain's prayer was not a comfort	B	1.35	.35
The Chaplain's visit(s) were not a comfort	B	1.56	.56
The Chaplain helped me use my faith/beliefs/values to cope with my feelings	C	2.50	7.50
The Chaplain helped me cope with my sense of loss	C	1.95	8.05

Outcome Research

Tables 8.7 and 8.8 demonstrate that pastoral care-givers make a significant contribution towards outcome research in both the general wards and the psychiatric wards with, as noted in the previous chapter, the results being more positive for patients in the general wards. The reader will recall that outcome is most important to patients in the general wards, while the person of the pastor with whom the patient relates is most important to patients suffering mental illness.

Table 8.7. Outcome Research (General Wards Sample)

	Distance from Ideal
'The Chaplain's visit(s) did not contribute to my readiness to go home'	.39
'The Chaplain's visit(s) did not make my hospitalization easier'	.47
'The Chaplain's visit(s) did not contribute to my getting better faster'	.54

These are ranked 30, 32, and 33 out of 35 constituent variables.

Table 8.8. Outcome Research (Psychiatric Unit Sample)

'The Chaplain's visit(s) did not contribute to my getting better faster'	.71
'The Chaplain's visit(s) did not make my hospitalization easier'	1.00
'The Chaplain's visit(s) did not contribute to my readiness to go home'	1.08

These are ranked 26, 30, and 32 out of the 35 constituent variables.

What Background Variables Significantly Influence the Scores?

Tables 8.9 and 8.10 report ANOVA F-scores for the association between the background variables and each sub-scale for the general wards and for the psychiatric wards respectively.

Table 8.9 demonstrates that, in the general wards, there is a relationship between Patient Satisfaction and Patient Age, between Patient Satisfaction and Gender, and between Patient Satisfaction and Frequency of Attendance at Community Worship.

Table 8.9. The Association between Background Variables and Sub-scale Scores in General Wards
In each case the F score is given first, with the significance in brackets.
Significance < .05 is flagged with *.

Background Variable	Sub-scales			
	A(Accpt)	B(Supp.)	C(Cope)	D(Priv.)
Patient Age:	ns	ns	*2.861(.029)	ns
Patient Gender:	ns	ns	ns	*5.932(.021)
Education:	ns	2.560(.074)	ns	ns
Patient Acuity:	ns	2.577(.059)	ns	ns
Distance from Hospital:	ns	1.387(.248)	ns	ns
Frequency of Visitors:	ns	ns	ns	1.489(.231)
Parish Pastor Visited:	2.142(.153)	ns	ns	2.498(.124)
Frequency of attendance at Community Religious Services:	*3.920(.031)	ns	ns	1.915(.165)
Marital Status:	ns	ns	1.803(.155)	ns
Attended Mass in Hospital:	ns	ns	ns	ns
Overall Satisfaction Level:	ns	ns	ns	1.001(.406)

Patient Satisfaction Scores and Patient Age. Patient Age is significantly related to sub-scale C, 'The Chaplain's Ministry to Help the Patient Cope' (F = *2.861; p = .029). Older patients cope better with illness. In ministering to younger patients, chaplains might keep the aspects of coping ministry to the fore. As age is a ratio variable (for which I used an appropriate statistical test) there is no cut off point.

Patient Satisfaction Scores and Gender. Patient gender is significantly related to sub-scale D, 'The Chaplain's Ministry to the Patient's Private Concerns' (F = *5.932; p = .021). Women appreciate ministry to private concerns more so than men.

Patient Satisfaction Scores and Frequency of Attendance at Community Religious Services. Patients' frequency of attendance at Community Religious Services is significantly related to sub-scale A, 'Acceptance of the Chaplain's Ministry' (F = *3.920; p = .031). Those who attend religious services more frequently are more accepting of the Chaplain's ministry.

Table 8.10 demonstrates that, in the psychiatric wards, there is a relationship between Patient Satisfaction and Patient Acuity, and between Patient Satisfaction and Frequency of Visitors.

Table 8.10. The Association between Background Variables and Sub-scale Scores in the Psychiatric Wards

Background Variable	Sub-scales			
	A(Accpt)	B(Supp.)	C(Cope)	D(Priv.)
Patient Age:	1.441(.299)	ns	ns	ns
Patient Gender:	ns	ns	2.403(.143)	ns
Education:	ns	ns	1.625(.236)	ns
Patient Acuity:	ns	*7.507(.004)	ns	ns
Distance from Hospital:	ns	1.628(.223)	ns	ns
Frequency of Visitors:	ns	ns	ns	*6.095(.027)
Parish Pastor Visited:	ns	ns	3.500(.082)	ns
Frequency of attendance at Community Religious Services:	1.179(.338)	ns	ns	ns
Relationship Status:	1.153(.301)	ns	ns	ns
Attended Mass in Hospital:	ns	ns	583(.458)	ns
Overall Satisfaction Level:	1.220(.362)	ns	ns	ns

Patient Satisfaction Scores and Patient Acuity. Patient acuity is significantly related to sub-scale B, 'The Chaplain's Supportive Ministry' (F = **7.507; p = .004). The more acutely ill patients appreciated the Chaplain's ministry more so than those who were less acutely ill. Chaplains might focus on the support aspects of ministry with those who are more acutely ill.

Patient Satisfaction Scores and Frequency of Visitors. Frequency of visitors is significantly related to sub-scale D, 'The Chaplain's Ministry to the Patient's Private Concerns' (F = *6.095). Patients who received more visitors appreciated ministry to private concerns more so than those who received fewer visitors.

Comparisons of Significant F Scores of Overall Sample, Sample from General Wards and Sample from Psychiatric Wards

Examination of Table 7.6 showed that in the overall sample three background variables were significantly related to sub-scales. These were, 'Patient Age' and 'The Chaplain's Ministry to Help the Patient Cope' (sub-scale C); 'Frequency of

Attendance at Community Worship' and Acceptance of the Chaplain's Ministry (sub-scale A);' and 'Overall Patient Satisfaction' and 'The Chaplain's Supportive Ministry' (sub-scale B).

Examination of Table 8.9 shows that, in the sample of general patients, three background variables were related to sub-scales. These were, 'Patient Age' and 'The Chaplain's Ministry to Help the Patient Cope' (sub-scale C); 'Patient Gender' and 'The Chaplain's Ministry to the Patient's Private Concerns' (sub-scale D); and 'Frequency of Attendance at Community Worship' and 'Acceptance of the Chaplain's Ministry' (sub-scale A). Patient gender was a significant background variable in the general hospital only.

Examination of Table 8.10 shows that, in the sample of psychiatric patients, two background variables were related to sub-scales. These were, 'Patient Acuity' and 'The Chaplain's Supportive Ministry' (sub-scale B); and 'Frequency of Visitors' and 'The Chaplain's Ministry to the Patients Private Concerns' (sub-scale D). Neither of these associations was significant in the sample of general patients or in the overall sample. It follows that they are most significant in relation to patients in the psychiatric units.

Conclusion

The patients in the general wards and the patients in the psychiatric wards who participated in the quantitative research both scored the four aspects of ministry in the same order, the most significant correlation being that between Patient Satisfaction and Ministry to the Patient's Private Concerns. Next was Acceptance of the Chaplain's Ministry, followed by The Chaplain's Ministry to Help the Patient Cope and The Chaplain's Supportive Ministry. In each aspect of ministry the satisfaction scores were higher for patients in the general wards.

In terms of the person of the pastor, both the general patients and the psychiatric patients ranked respect, spiritual sensitivity, and competency as the important qualities of the Chaplain. However, the general patients ranked 'competency' as the most important quality, followed by 'respect' and 'spiritual sensitivity,' while the psychiatric patients ranked 'respect' first, followed by 'spiritual sensitivity' and 'competency.' This is consistent with the finding that, of the three areas considered namely, the person of the pastor, the skills of ministry, and the outcome of ministry, patients in the general wards ranked outcome as most important, while the patients in the psychiatric wards ranked the person of the pastor as paramount. This is consistent with the finding that outcome research variables yielded higher scores from the general patients.

Active listening was the most important skill for all patients, with those in the general wards also appreciating appropriate prayer. The most appreciated outcomes of ministry for all patients were 'help with loneliness,' 'help to feel God's care,' 'help to feel more relaxed,' and 'comfort (of) the Chaplain's prayer.' Patients in the general wards appreciated private prayer, while those in the psychiatric wards appreciated formal prayer more.

In relation to background variables, there was no statistically significant background variable that was common to both the general patients and the psychiatric patients. For the general patients, the background variables that correlated significantly with Patient Satisfaction were 'Patient Age,' 'Gender,' and 'Frequency of Attendance at Community Worship.' For the psychiatric patients, the significant background variables were 'Patient Acuity' and 'Frequency of Visitors.'

Overall, both general and psychiatric patients agreed about the more important aspects of ministry, with some differences in emphases. The most noteworthy difference was the greater emphasis placed by the general patients on the 'outcome' of ministry, and the greater emphasis placed on 'the person of the pastor' by patients suffering from mental illness.

Chapter 9

The Theory and the Findings

The Problem Restated

This work originated in my desire to inquire about the contribution of pastoral care to the holistic care of acutely ill adult hospital in-patients. This is my life's work and I was searching for the deeper meaning of it. I wanted to know what aspects of pastoral care were most helpful and contributed most to holistic care, and most importantly, I wanted to know 'why?' and 'how?' these particular aspects of pastoral care contributed. This search embraced both theology and psychology. I searched in theology for the deeper meaning and for an answer to the 'why?,' and in psychology for an answer to the 'how?'

This study is based on the theory that pastoral relatedness is the essence of pastoral care. Pastoral relatedness is that special quality of the pastoral relationship that communicates God's care to those who suffer. The nature of God is that God cares for each person. Persons experience this care in their deeper spiritual selves. Psychology enables us to understand how this might happen. This study posits that pastoral relatedness is the basis of high satisfaction levels with pastoral care.

The Theory and the Findings

This study found that there was a high level of patient satisfaction with pastoral care, the highest correlation being that between Patient Satisfaction and the Chaplain's Ministry to the Patient's Private Concerns. The formulation of the theory, utilizing the resources of theology and psychology, sought to demonstrate that quality pastoral relatedness, which enables people to share their private concerns and have them heard, is the basis for this high level of patient satisfaction.

The Person and the Skills of the Pastor. The person of Jesus was central to his pastoral care. The nature and essence of Jesus' pastoral care, through shepherding and healing, was a trusting relationship, based on the relationship between the Father and Son. Modern pastoral care writers agree that the person of the pastor is central in modern pastoral care. The pastoral care-giver must have the ability to be in pastoral relationships, which bear the quality of pastoral relatedness. Radar, Estadt and Moorman, and Nouwen outlined the personality characteristics and skills that make for effectiveness in pastoral care. An effective pastoral care-giver approaches the other with a sense of mystery, is focused towards the personal, and has an understanding of persons. This research found that effective pastoral care-givers are respectful, spiritually sensitive, and competent. Estadt and Moorman stated that an effective pastoral counselor has the ability to communicate with the other in a therapeutic relationship. This study found that an effective pastoral care-giver possesses the skill of active listening, which conveys care and understanding, thus enabling and facilitating a person to share his/her private concerns.

The person and the skills of the pastor enable pastoral relatedness. The constituent variables within sub-scales D and A,

'Ministry to the Patient's Private Concerns' and 'Acceptance of the Chaplain's Ministry' respectively, measure patient satisfaction with the person of the pastor and his/her skills. These sub-scales measure the pastor's ability to create a high quality pastoral relationship. This research found these sub-scales to be prioritized first and second in order of importance by the patients. Crosstabs revealed that all participants experienced the chaplains as compassionate and possessing a judgement free attitude, both aspects of pastoral relatedness. For the patients who participated in this research, pastoral relatedness was the essence of pastoral care. Furthermore, each of the patients who participated in the qualitative research named listening and understanding as the essence of pastoral care. These qualities are integral components of pastoral relatedness.

The responses to the questions, 'What was most helpful about the Chaplain's visit(s)?' and 'the Chaplain's most important quality?' with 'Listening' and 'Good Listener' named as the most important skill and quality respectively confirm that active listening is the most appreciated skill.

In relation to the question about preference for a female chaplain, male chaplain, or ordained chaplain, the spontaneous response of many participants that the person of the pastor was a most important factor confirms the centrality of the person of the pastor for pastoral ministry.

These two findings confirm that the training of Chaplains should continue to emphasize the self-development of the pastor, competency of the skills, and the integration of the two.

Theology and psychology are integrated. Lee E. Snook uses the concept of 'relatedness' to describe the relationships within the Trinity. He is at pains to convey that this means "intimate, not remote; internal, not external."[1] The Roman Catholic theologian Walter J. Burghardt and the Protestant theologian David Belgum stated that personal pastoral relationship is the most important aspect of pastoral care. It is through this relationship that the blocks are removed and grace is allowed to flow more freely. Psychologically this allows the ego to descend into and live in the deep mind and find inner peace.

Person and skills are integrated. The healing is in the trusting relationship enabled by the person of the pastor. Each of the patients who participated in the qualitative research affirmed the centrality of the 'warm and trusting' pastoral relationship, which enabled and facilitated sharing of their private concerns.

The Outcome of Pastoral Ministry. A respectful, spiritually sensitive, and competent pastor utilizing the skills of active listening to patients' private concerns enables positive outcomes of pastoral ministry. Sub-scales B and C, 'The Chaplain's Supportive Ministry' and 'The Chaplain's Ministry to Help the Patient Cope,' measured these outcomes. In relation to the Chaplain's supportive ministry, those more satisfied with their overall hospital stay experienced the Chaplain's supportive ministry as more helpful than those less satisfied did. The implication of this is that Chaplains should attend to the supportive aspects of pastoral care, as outlined in Sub-scale B of the questionnaire, when ministering to those who are less satisfied with their hospital stay.

Kearney stated that spiritual pain may cause a person to struggle with such questions as 'what is the meaning of this?' and 'why me?' The person may be agitated and restless deep within him or herself. Some of the spiritual struggle may be expressed religiously, 'is God punishing me?' 'what kind of God is this? These questions challenge the Chaplain to help the patient cope. This research found that, while the more difficult skills demanded for this deeper ministry were called for less often than those for supportive ministry, that they were most important when required.[2] The findings show that the Chaplain's Ministry to Help the Patient Cope rated higher than the Chaplain's Supportive Ministry demonstrating that the chaplains possessed the necessary skills for this ministry. The discussion in chapter seven on the outcome of pastoral ministry revealed that ministry, which helped patients cope with loss, was most helpful to the significant minority of patients who required it. Utilization of the patient's faith/beliefs/values was most important in enabling him/her cope with loss ($r = .889$; $p < .000$; $n = 17$). This was more pronounced for patients suffering from mental illness. It seems that faith/beliefs/values are crucial factors in enabling people discover meaning in loss.

Outcome Research. In relation to outcome research it is noteworthy that the pastoral relationship with the Chaplain and the Chaplain spending adequate time with the patient contributed significantly to the patient's 'getting better faster.'[3] This supports my theory that pastoral relatedness, which is central to quality pastoral care, is an essential aspect of quality pastoral care.

Sharing of private concerns with the Chaplain and the Chaplain spending adequate time with the patient contributed significantly to patients' 'readiness to go home.'[4] This further confirms the significance of ministry to the patient's private concerns.

Overall, these findings confirm that quality pastoral care includes sharing of private concerns in the context of pastoral relatedness. This demands spending adequate time with the patient.

Background Variables. In relation to the Background Variables, we can predict that older people will cope better with illness, and that those who attend community worship regularly are more likely to accept the Chaplain's ministry. Frequency of visitors is generally beneficial to hospital patients.

This study found that patients in the general wards received more visitors than patients in the psychiatric wards (Means and SD's: General wards: 1.18[.39]; Psychiatric wards: 1.62[.50]). Perhaps lesser social support places persons at greater risk of mental illness? Or, perhaps, there is still some stigma attached to mental illness that causes patients to want to conceal their illness, or makes it more difficult or more embarrassing for visitors to visit? I believe both contentions to be true. It follows that Chaplains should be aware that visitors would generally benefit patients suffering mental illness. Chaplains might encourage people to visit, and possibly make connections for such people with churches or parish visitors. However, it is important that, as in all visits to patients in hospitals, visitors be alert for signs that the patient may not desire or be able for a visit at any particular time. The finding that those who received more visitors experienced the Chaplain's visit(s) as more hopeful (r = **.409; n = 42) indicates an important outcome, as does the finding that mentally ill patients who received more visitors availed more of ministry to private concerns (F = *6.095). The frequency of visitors probably helps a person in relation to social support, and self-esteem.

The Importance of Continuity with the same Chaplain. This research found that continuity with the same Chaplain is important. The findings of the quantitative research were confirmed in the qualitative interviews, during which each interviewee stated that continuity with the same Chaplain was important to him/her. This confirms that Heads of Pastoral Care Teams with responsibility for assigning chaplains within a hospital should assign team members to specific wards and/or specialties, and assign the same Chaplain to wards that cater for cognate disciplines.

Conclusion

The findings of this study affirm for me that pastoral relatedness is the essence of pastoral care. They confirm my personal theology of Pastoral Care, which integrates the person, the skills, and the outcome of pastoral care. The love of God, revealed in Jesus Christ and with us through the Holy Spirit, motivates a pastoral care-giver to reach out to people, and through the medium of pastoral relatedness, the pastor communicates God's love to those who suffer. This enables the person to remove blocks in relating to God and others, and thus experience the freedom of the Son of God and move towards salvation.

Notes:

1. Lee E. Snook, "A Primer on the Trinity: Keeping Our Theology Christian," *Word and World* 2 no. 1 (1982): 6.
2. See Table 7.3 p.91 for percentage answering for each constituent variable.
3. The correlation between pastoral relationship and 'getting better faster' was r = .481; n = 36. The correlation between spending adequate time with the patient and 'getting better faster' was r = -.445; n =35).
4. The correlation between sharing of private concerns and 'readiness to go home' was r = **-.503; n = 30. The correlation between spending adequate time with the patient and 'readiness to go home' was r = *-.410; n = 29.

Appendix A

Questionaire - Patient Satisfaction with Pastoral Care

These items concern how well the Chaplain and his/her visit met your needs in his/her pastoral visit(s) with you. Please circle the best answer for each statement. If a statement does not apply to you or to your experience, please circle 'Not Applicable.'

PLEASE CIRCLE YOUR ANSWER

Section A: Acceptance of the Chaplain's Ministry

	Strongly Disagree	Mildly Disagree	Mildly Agree	Strongly Agree	Not Applicable
The Chaplain's visit(s) made me tired	1	2	3	4	0
The Chaplain's visit(s) were too long	1	2	3	4	0
The Chaplain's visit(s) scared me	1	2	3	4	0
The Chaplain's visit(s) frustrated me	1	2	3	4	0
The Chaplain talked too much	1	2	3	4	0
I did not feel respected by the Chaplain	1	2	3	4	0

Section B: The Chaplain's Supportive Ministry

	Strongly Disagree	Mildly Disagree	Mildly Agree	Strongly Agree	Not Applicable
After talking with the Chaplain, I did not feel any better about my problem	1	2	3	4	0
The Chaplain's visit(s) did not help relieve my worries about my problem	1	2	3	4	0
The Chaplain's visit(s) were not a comfort to me	1	2	3	4	0
The Chaplain's visit(s) did not make my hospitalization easier	1	2	3	4	0
The Chaplain's visit(s) did not help me adjust to the medical situation	1	2	3	4	0
The Chaplain's visits(s) did not help me overcome my fears	1	2	3	4	0
The Chaplain's visit(s) did not help my loneliness	1	2	3	4	0
The Chaplain's visit(s) did not give me strength to go on	1	2	3	4	0
The Chaplain's visit(s) did not help me feel more relaxed	1	2	3	4	0
The Chaplain's visit(s) did not help me feel God's care	1	2	3	4	0
The Chaplain's visit(s) did not help me stay in touch with my faith	1	2	3	4	0
The Chaplain's visit(s) did not help me feel more hopeful	1	2	3	4	0
The chaplain's visit(s) did not contribute to my getting better faster	1	2	3	4	0
The Chaplain's visit(s) did not contribute to my readiness to go home	1	2	3	4	0
The Chaplain did not help me face difficult issues connected with my situation	1	2	3	4	0
The Chaplain's prayer did not comfort me	1	2	3	4	0

Section C: The Chaplain's Ministry to Help the Patient Cope

	Strongly Disagree	Mildly Disagree	Mildly Agree	Strongly Agree	Not Applicable
My need for the sacraments was fulfilled	1	2	3	4	0
The Mass in the Chapel/Day Room helped meet my needs	1	2	3	4	0
The Chaplain helped me use my faith/ beliefs/values to cope with my feelings	1	2	3	4	0
The Chaplain helped me cope with my sense of loss	1	2	3	4	0
The Chaplain helped me with guilt feelings	1	2	3	4	0
The Chaplain helped me with an ethical problem	1	2	3	4	0
The Chaplain helped me find meaning in my situation	1	2	3	4	0
The Chaplain helped me co-operate with the doctors and nurses	1	2	3	4	0

Section D: The Chaplain's Ministry to the Patient's Private Concerns

	Strongly Disagree	Mildly Disagree	Mildly Agree	Strongly Agree	Not Applicable
The Chaplain was a person of spiritual sensitivity	1	2	3	4	0
The Chaplain seemed to know what s/he was doing during our visit(s)	1	2	3	4	0
The Chaplain spent adequate time with me	1	2	3	4	0
The Chaplain was really listening to me	1	2	3	4	0
I felt free to share my private concerns with the Chaplain	1	2	3	4	0

- What was most helpful about the Chaplain's visit(s)? (CIRCLE ONE ONLY). Please comment.

    1. Listening
    2. Being with me
    3. Understanding
    4. Kindness
    5. Sensitivity
    6. Prayer
    7. Sacrament
    8. Other

- What was most unhelpful about the Chaplain's visit(s)? (CIRCLE ONE ONLY). Please comment.

    1. Did not listen
    2. Rushed
    3. Didn't understand me
    4. Didn't seem to know what to say or do
    5. Insensitivity
    6. Other
    7. Nothing

- What important positive qualities did the chaplain possess?

    1. Trustworthiness
    2. Good listener
    3. Kindness
    4. Prayerfulness
    5. Warmth
    6. Compassion
    7. Judgement free attitude
    8. Sensitivity
    9. Genuineness
    10. Not Applicable

- Which was the most important quality? Please comment.

- What was the Chaplain's weakness?
  (CIRCLE ONE ONLY). Please comment.
  1. Poor listener
  2. Lack of confidence
  3. Uncomfortable in his/her role
  4. Distant
  5. Judgmental attitude
  6. Insensitive
  7. Insincerity
  8. Not Applicable

- Would you prefer
  (CIRCLE ONE ONLY). Please comment.

  1. Female Chaplain?
  2. Male Chaplain?
  3. Ordained Chaplain?

- Was Chaplain
  (CIRCLE ONE ONLY). Please comment.

  1. Staff Chaplain?
  2. Chaplain-in-Training?
  3. Met both
  4. Don't know

- How important is continuity with the same chaplain?
  (CIRCLE ONE ONLY). Please comment.

  1. Very important
  2. Important
  3. Somewhat important
  4. Not at all important

- How would you describe your relationship with the Chaplain whom you know best? (CIRCLE ONE ONLY). Please comment.
  1. Warm
  2. Somewhat warm
  3. Somewhat distant
  4. Distant

- How important for good pastoral care is your pastoral relationship with the chaplain? (CIRCLE ONE ONLY)

    1. Most important
    2. Important
    3. Somewhat important
    4. Not at all important

1. Your age:____________ years.

2. Are you? (Circle one)

    1. Male
    2. Female

3. Are you? (Circle one)

    1. Single
    2. Widow(er)
    3. Divorced
    4. Separated
    5. Married
    6. In committed relationship

4. Have you completed? (Circle one)

    1. National school
    2. Secondary school
    3. Third level (without degree)
    4. Third level (with degree)

5. How ill were you when admitted to the hospital? (Circle one)

    1. Not very ill
    2. A little ill
    3. Somewhat ill
    4. Very ill
    5. Extremely ill

6. How far from your home is the hospital? (Circle one)

    1. Less than 40 miles
    2. More than 40 miles

7. How often do you have visitors while in the hospital? (Circle one)

    1. Almost daily
    2. 3 – 4 times a week or less

8. Did a pastor of your parish visit you in the hospital? (Circle one)

    1. Yes
    2. No

9. If 'no' would you have welcomed such a visit? (Circle one)

    (a) Yes
    (b) No

10. How frequently do you usually attend religious services? (Circle one)

    1. Regularly (once a week or more)
    2. Occasionally or only on special days
    3. Not at all

11. Did you attend Mass in the hospital? (Circle one)

    1. Yes
    2. No

12. If yes - in Chapel? [ ] (Tick one)
day room TV? [ ]

13. Please tell us how satisfied you were with your overall hospital stay
(CIRCLE ONE ONLY). Please comment.

1. Extremely satisfied
2. Somewhat satisfied
3. Neutral
4. Somewhat dissatisfied
5. Extremely dissatisfied

COMMENTS: Please uses this space for any comments you wish to make about your experience with the Hospital Chaplain(s).

Thank you very much for your response

Bibliography

Acklin M., E. Brown, and P. Mauger. "The Role of Religious Values in Coping with Cancer." *Journal of Religion and Health* 22 (1983): 322-33.

Ahlskog, Gary. "They Had to Beg Us to Pray: Reflection on the Undesirability of Clinical Pastoral Education." *The Journal of Pastoral Care* 47, no. 2 (1993): 179-87.

Allison, David W. "Communicating Clinical Pastoral Assessments with the Healthcare Team." *The Journal of Pastoral Care* 46, no. 3 (1992): 273-80.

Amundsen, Darrell W. "The Medieval Catholic Tradition." In *Caring and Curing: Health and Medicine in the Western Religious Traditions*, 65-107. New York: MacMillan Publishing Co., 1986.

Amundsen, Darrell W., and Gary B. Ferngren. "The Early Christian Tradition." In *Caring and Curing: Health and Medicine in the Western Religious Traditions*, 40-64. New York: MacMillan Publishing Co., 1986.

Anderson, George Christian. "Partnership of Theologians and Psychiatrists." *Journal of Religion and Health* 3, no.1 (1963): 56-69.

Ashley, Benedict, and Kevin O'Rourke. *Health Care Ethics: A Theological Analysis*, 4th ed. Washington DC: Georgetown University Press, 1997.

Association of Clinical Pastoral Education. "CPE – 50 Years – Learning with Living Human Documents." *News* 8 no. 1 (1975): 1-5.
Autton, Norman. *Pastoral Care In Hospitals*. London: SPCK, 1968.
Ballard, Paul H. "Pastoral Studies. "In *A Dictionary of Pastoral Care*, ed. Alastair V. Campbell, 200. London: SPCK, 1987.
Bascom, G .S. "Physical, emotional, and cognitive care of dying patients." Bulletin of the Menninger Clinic 48 (1984): 351-6.
Bayley, Corrine. "The Chaplain and Ethical Decision Making." In *Health Care Ministry: A Handbook for Chaplains*, eds. Helen Hayes and Cornelius van der Poel, 22-36. New York: Paulist Press, 1990.
Behen, Joseph M., and James R. Rodrigue, "Predictors of Coping Strategies among Adults with Cancer." *Psychological Reports* 74 no. 1 (1994): 43-8.
Belgum, David. "The Theology of Pastoral Care." *The Lutheran Quarterly* 11, no. 3 (1959): 207-21.
Bellamy, Peter. "Hospital Chaplaincy." In *A Dictionary of Pastoral Care*, ed. Alastair V. Campbell, 117-8. London: SPCK, 1987.
Belleamare, D. "AIDS: The Challenge to Pastoral Care." *Journal of Palliative Care* 4, no. 4 (1988): 58-60.
Benner Verna and Harry Green. "Spiritual Well-Being: A Predictor of Hardiness in Patients with Acquired Immunodeficiency Syndrome." In *Spiritual Needs and Pastoral Services: Readings in Research*, ed. Larry VandeCreek, 231-54. Decatur, GA: Journal of Pastoral Care Publications, 1995. Originally published in *Journal of Professional Nursing* 8 no. 4 (1992): 209-20.
Benson, H. "The Faith Factor." *American Health* 5 (1984): 50-3.
Benson, P., and B. Spilka. "God Image as a Function of Self-Esteem and Locus of Control." *Journal for the Scientific Study of Religion* 12 (1973): 297-310.
Berwick, Donald, M. "Continuous Improvement As An Ideal in Health Care." *The New England Journal of Medicine* 320 no. 1 (1989): 53-6.
Beuchner, Frederick. *Telling Secrets: A Memoir*. San Francisco: Harper Collins, 1991.
Bielby, Donald. "Quality Assurance in Pastoral Care in Hospitals." *Pastoral Sciences* 5, (1986), 65-86.
Bohne, J. "Ministry Issues for Chaplains." *Pastoral Psychology* 34, no. 3 (1986): 173-92.
Boisen, Anton T. *The Exploration of the Inner World: A Study of Mental Disorder and Religious Experience*. New York: Willett, Claire and Company, 1936.
________. *Out of the Depths, an autobiographical study of mental disorder and religious experience*. New York, Harper, 1960.
Bonacker, Ralph D. "Clinical Training for the Pastoral Ministry: Purposes & Methods." *The Journal of Pastoral Care* 14, no. 1 (1960): 1-12.
Boyer, Ralph E. "An Evaluation into the Nature and Use of the Concept of the Healing Team in Fairview Park Hospital." Masters thesis, Oberlin Graduate School of Theology, 1962.

Brakeman, Lyn G. "Theology as a Diagnostic Tool in the Assessment of Spiritual Health." *The Journal of Pastoral Care* 49, no. 1 (1995): 29-37.

Brody, Howard. *Stories of Sickness*. New Haven: Yale University Press, 1987.

Browning, Don S. "Ethics and Pastoral Care." In *Dictionary of Pastoral Care and Counseling*, ed. Rodney J. Hunter, 364-66. Nashville: Abingdon Press, 1990.

________. *A Fundamental Practical Theology: Descriptive & Strategic Proposals*. Minneapolis: Fortress Press, 1991.

________. "Pastoral Theology in a Pluralistic Age." *Pastoral Psychology* 29 (fall 1980).

________, ed. *Religious and Ethical Factors in Psychiatric Practice*. Chicago: Nelson-Hall, 1990.

Bruder, Ernest E. "Clinical Pastoral Training in Preparation for the Pastoral Ministry." *The Journal of Pastoral Care* 16 no. 1 (1962): 25-33.

Buber, Martin, *I and Thou*. New York: Charles Scribner's Sons, 1958.

Bueschner, Frederick. *Telling Secrets: A Memoir*. San Francisco: Harper Collins, 1991.

Bufford, R. K., R. F. Paloutzian, and C. W. Ellison. "Norms for the Spiritual Well-Being Scale." *Journal of Psychology and Theology* 19 (1991): 56-70.

Burck, J. R., and Hunter, R. J. "Pastoral Theology, Protestant." In *Dictionary of Pastoral Care and Counseling*, ed. Rodney J. Hunter, 867-72. Nashville: Abingdon Press, 1990.

Burghardt, Walter J. "Towards A Theology of Pastoral Care. " n. p., n. d.

Burton, Laurel Arthur. ed. "Chaplaincy with Protestant Patients." In *Chaplaincy Services in Contemporary Health Care*, 99-103. Schaumburg, Ill.: The College of Chaplains, 1992.

_______. "Chaplaincy with Roman Catholic Patients." In *Chaplaincy Services in Contemporary Healthcare*, 95-8. Schaumburg, Ill.: The College of Chaplains, 1992.

________. "Establishing and Implementing a Chaplaincy Program." In *Chaplaincy Services in Contemporary Healthcare*, 23-28. Schaumburg, Ill. The College of Chaplains, 1972.

________. *Pastoral Paradigms: Christian Ministry in a Pluralistic Culture*. n. p.: The Alban Institute, 1988.

________. "Personnel and Facilities for Pastoral Care." In *Chaplaincy Services in Contemporary Healthcare*, 29-32. Schaumburg, Ill: The College of Chaplains, 1972.

________. "The Professional Health Care Chaplain." In *Chaplaincy Services in Contemporary Health Care*,1-6. Schaumburg, Ill.: The College of Chaplains, 1992.

________. "The Work of the Hospital Chaplain." In *Chaplaincy Services in Contemporary Healthcare*, 15-20. Schaumburg, Ill.: The College of Chaplains, 1972.

Burton, Laurel Arthur, and Donald F. Philips." The Role of the Chaplain in Ethical Decision Making." In *Chaplaincy Services in Contemporary Health Care*, ed. Laurel Arthur Burton, 43-50. Schaumburg, Illinois: The College of Chaplains, 1992.

Buryska, James. "Pastoral Care Administration." In *Health Care Ministry: A Handbook for Chaplains*, eds. Helen Hayes and Cornelius van der Poel, 65-78. New York: Paulist Press, 1990.

Byrd, Randolf C. "Positive Therapeutic Effects of Intercessory Prayer in a Coronary Care Unit Population." In *Spiritual Needs and Pastoral Services: Readings in Research*, ed. Larry VandeCreek, 67-77. Decatur, GA: Journal of Pastoral Care Publications, 1995. Originally published in *Southern Medical Journal* 81 no. 7 (1988): 826-9.

Calhoun, Gerard. *Pastoral Companionship*. New York: Paulist Press, 1986.

Campbell, Alastair V. "Pastoral Care, Nature of." In *A Dictionary of Pastoral Care*, 188-90. London: SPCK, 1987.

Cannon, John M. "Pastoral Care for Families of the Mentally Ill." *The Journal of Pastoral Care* 44, no. 3 (1990): 213-221.

Carey, Lindsay B., Rosalie Aroni and Allen R. Edwards, "Medical Ethics and the Role of Hospital Chaplains: A Case Study Research Report." *Ministry, Society and Theology* 10 no. 2 (1996): 66-79.

Carey, Raymond G. "Chaplaincy: Component of Total Patient Care?" *Hospitals*, July 16,1973, 166-72.

________. "Hospital Chaplains: Who Needs Them? A Study of the Role Expectations & Role Value of the Chaplains at Lutheran General Hospital, Park Ridge, Illinois." Park Ridge, Illinois. Unpublished Report, 1972.

________. "Change in Perceived Need, Value & Role of Hospital Chaplains." In *Hospital Ministry: The Role of the Chaplain Today*, ed. Lawrence E. Holst, 28-41. New York: Crossroad, 1985.

Carroll, John T. "Sickness and Healing in the New Testament Gospels." *Interpretation* 49 (1995): 130-42.

Carson, V., K. L. Soeken, and P.M. Grimm. "Hope and Its Relationship to Spiritual Well-Being." *Journal of Psychology and Theology* 16 (1988): 159-67.

Carson, V., K. L. Soeken, J. Shanty, and L. Terry. "Hope and Spiritual Well-Being: Essentials for Living with Aids." *Perspectives in Psychiatric Care* 26 no. 2 (1990): 28-34.

Carter, Sara. "Quality Assurance. " In *Health Care Ministry: A Handbook for Chaplains*, ed. Helen Hayes and Cornelius J. van der Poel, 79-87. New York: Paulist Press, Integration Books, 1990.

Cassell, J. "The Contribution of the Social Environment to Host Resistance." *American Journal of Epidemiology* 104 (1976): 107-23.

Cassidy, Michael. "The Search for Ministry Effectiveness in the Modern World." *The Gospel in the Modern World*, ed. Martyn Eden and David F. Wells, 236-72. Downers Grove, Illinois: Inter-Varsity Press, 1991.

Cassidy, Sheila. *Sharing the Darkness: The Spirituality of Caring*. London: Darton, Longman and Todd, 1988.

Catholic Health Association. *Guidelines for Evaluating Departments of Pastoral Care*. St. Louis, MO: Catholic Health Association, 1984.

Cheston, Sharon, and Robert J. Wicks, eds. *Essentials for Chaplains*. New York: Paulist Press, 1993.

Chirban, John T., ed. *Health and Faith: Medical, Psychological and Religious Dimensions*. Lenham, MD: University Press of America, 1991.

________. "Healing and Spirituality." *Pastoral Psychology* 40, no. 4 (1992): 235-44.

Ciampa, Ralph C. "God-Talk in Pastoral Care: Three Dimensions of the Pastoral Encounter." *The Journal of Pastoral Care* 30, no. 1 (1976): 27-34.

Cleary, Francis X. "The Church in Health Care: Reflection and Projections." *Hospital Progress* 63, (January 1982), 38-45.

Cleary, P. D. "Patient Satisfaction as an Indicator of Quality Care." *Inquiry* 25 (spring 1988): 25-36.

Clebsch, William A., and Charles R. Jaekle, *Pastoral Care in Historical Perspective*. Eaglewood Cliffs, New Jersey: Prentice Hall, Inc., 1994.

Cobb, John B. *Theology and Pastoral Care*. Philadelphia: Fortress Press, 1977.

Cobb, S. "Social Support as a Moderator of Life Stress." *Psychosomatic Medicine* 38 (1976): 300-14.

Cohen, Laurence, Gerald A. Specter, and William L. Claiborne, eds. *Crisis Intervention*. New York: Human Sciences Press, 1983.

Cooper, Robert M. "Intimacy." *St Luke's Journal of Theology* 30 no. 2 (1987): 113-124.

Coll, Regina. *Supervision of Ministry Students*. Collegeville, MN: Liturgical Press, 1992.

Collins, Mary, and David N. Power, eds. *The Pastoral Care of the Sick*. London: SCM, 1991.

COMISS/JCAPS: Standards For Accrediting Pastoral Services. Milwaukee, WI: Joint Commission on Accreditation of Pastoral Services (JCAPS), 1996.

Conrad, N.L. "Spiritual Support for the Dying." *Nursing Clinics of North America* 20, (1985): 415-26.

Conwill, W. L. "Chronic pain conceptualization and religious interpretation." *Journal of Religion and Health* 25 (1986): 46-50.

Cotterell, Dorothy, and William F. Nisi. "Clinical Pastoral Education." In *Health CareMinistry: A Handbook for Chaplains*, eds. Helen Hayes and Cornelius J Van der Poel. New Jersey: Paulist Press, 1990.

Coyle, Tom, ed. *Christian Ministry to the Sick*. London: Geoffrey Chapman, 1986.

Creighton, J. D. "Pastoral Care: History-The Roman Catholic Tradition." In *A Dictionary of Pastoral Care*, ed. Alastair V. Campbell, 195-6. London: SPCK, 1987.

Crag, S., and L. Leaven. "Religious Identity and Response to Serious Illness: A Report on Heart Patients." *Social Science and Medicine* 6 (1972): 17-32.

Cutri, Sister Mary Paul. "The Touch of God: Human/Divine Intimacy." *Spiritual Life* 30 (fall 1984): 155-164.

Dafter, Roger E. "Why 'Negative' Emotions can sometimes be Positive: the Spectrum Model of Emotions and their Role in Mind-body Healing." *Advances* 12 no. 2 (1996): 6-19.

Davies, Richard E. *Handbook For Doctor of Ministry Projects: An Approach to Structured Observation of Ministry*. New York: University Press of America, 1984.

De Blase, Richard R. "Intimacy in Pastoral Care." *Human Development* 7, no. 2 (1986): 27-31.

DeLong, William R. "Organ Donation and Hospital Chaplains." In *Spiritual Needs and Pastoral Services: Readings in Research*, ed. Larry VandeCreek, 125-36. Decatur, GA, Journal of Pastoral Care Publications, 1995. Originally published in *Transplantation* 50 no. 1 (1990): 25-9.

Derricks, Paul E. "Instruments Used to Measure Change in Students Preparing for Ministry: A Summary of Research on Clinical Pastoral Education Students." *The Journal of Pastoral Care* 44, no. 4 (1990): 343-56.

The Doctor and The Minister: A Discussion on Medical-Clerical Co-Operation for the Good of the Sick. Sydney, Australia: Council of Churches, 1960.

Dodds, Michael J. "Ultimacy and Intimacy. Aquinas on the Relation between God and the World" In *Ordo Sapientiae Et Amoris*, ed. Carlos-Josephat Pinto de Oliveira, 211-227. Fribourg: Universitaires Fribourg Suisse, 1993.

Doehring, Carrie. *Taking Care: Monitoring Power Dynamics and Relational Boundries in Pastoral Care and Counseling*. Nashville: Abingdon Press, 1995.

Donabedian, A. "Quality Assessment and Assurance: Unity of Purpose, Diversity of Means." *Inquiry* 25 (spring 1988): 173-92.

Dossey, Larry, MD. Healing Words: *The Power of Prayer and the Practice of Medicine*. New York: Harper Collins, 1993.

Draper, Edgar, *Psychiatry and Pastoral Care*. Philadephia: Fortress Press, 1965.

Driscoll, Joseph J. "Chaplains Treat What Doctors Can't: Heart, Soul." *National Catholic Reporter*, October 28, 1994, 18-9.

Draper, Edgar, and Bevan Steedman. "Assessment in Pastoral Care." In *Clinical Handbook of Pastoral Counseling*. Vol.1, ed. R. Wicks. n. p., 1993.

Droege, Thomas A. *The Faith Factor in Healing*. Philadelphia: Trinity Press International, 1991.

Duckro, Paul N., and Magaletta, Philip R. "The Effect of Prayer on Physical Health: Experimental Evidence." *Journal of Religion and Health* 33 no. 3 (1994): 211-9.

Duffy, R. "Roman Catholic Pastoral Care." In *Dictionary of Pastoral Care and Counseling*, ed. Rodney J. Hunter, 1093-95. Nashville: Abingdon Press, 1990.

Dykstra, Robert C. "Intimate Strangers: The Role of the Hospital Chaplain in Situations of Sudden Traumatic Loss." *The Journal of Pastoral Care* 44, no. 2 (1990): 139-52.

Dyson, A. O. "Pastoral Theology." In A *Dictionary of Pastoral Care*, ed. Alastair V. Campbell, 201-2. London: SPCK, 1987.

Edlin, Gordon, and Eric Golanty. *Health and Wellness: a holistic approach*. Boston, MA: Jones and Bartlett, 1985.

Egan, Gerard. *The Skilled Helper: A Problem-Management Approach to Healing*, 6th ed. Pacific Grove, CA: Brooks/Cole Publishing Co. 1998.

Eimer, Kenneth W. "The Assessment and Treatment of the Religiously Concerned Psychiatric Patient." *The Journal of Pastoral Care* 43 no. 3 (1989): 231-41.

Einerson, R. "Productivity Measures for Chaplains: How to develop a database documentation system." *The CareGiver Journal* 7 no. 4 (1990): 24-36.

Eisner, Betty G., and Humphrey Osmond. "The Sick Role vs. the Dying Role." *Advances* 12 no. 2 (1996): 67-70.

Ellison, C. W. "Spiritual Well-Being: Conceptualization and Measurement." *Journal of Psychology and Theology* 11 (1983): 330-40.

________. "Spirituality: A Systemic View." *Journal of Psychology and Theology* 17, no. 3 (1989): 158-67.

Engel, George L. "The Clinical Application of the Biopsychosocial Model" *American Journal of Psychiatry* 137 no.5 (1980): 535-43.

Engel, George L. "The Need for a New Medical Model: A Challenge for Biomedicine." In *Concepts of Health and Disease: Interdisciplinary, Perspectives*. ed. Arthur L. Coaplan, H. Tristram Engelhardt Jr. and James J. McCartney, 589-605. London: Addison-Wesley Publishing Co., 1981.

Estadt, Barry, John Compton and Melvin C. Blanchette, eds. *The Art of Clinical Supervision: A Pastoral Counseling Perspective*. New York: Paulist Press, 1987.

Estadt, Barry, and William J. Moorman. "Pastoral Counseling in the Health Care Setting." In *Health Care Ministry: A Handbook for Chaplains*, eds. Helen Hayes and Cornelius J. van der Poel, 167-87. New York: Paulist Press, 1990.

Faber, Heije. *Pastoral Care in the Modern Hospital*. Philadelphia: The Westminster Press, 1971.

Favazza, Armando R. "Modern Christian Healing of Mental Illness." *American Journal of Psychiatry* 139, no. 6 (1984): 728-35.

Fichter, Joseph Henry. *Religion and Pain: The Spiritual Dimensions of Health Care*. New York: Crossroad, 1981.

Fichter, Joseph Henry. *Healing Ministries: Conversations on the Spiritual Dimension of Healthcare*. New York: Paulist Press, 1986.

Fitchett, George. *Spiritual Assessment in Pastoral Care: A Guide to Selected Resources*. Decatur, GA: Journal of Pastoral Care Publications, Inc., Monograph No.4, 1993.

Fitchett, George, and George T. Gray. "Evaluating the Outcome of Clinical Pastoral Education: A Test of the Clinical Ministry Assessment Profile." *Journal of Supervision and Training In Ministry* 15 (1994): 3-22

Florell, J. "Crisis Intervention in Orthopedic Surgery-Empirical Evidence of the Effectiveness of a Chaplain Working with Surgery Patients." In *Spiritual Needs and Pastoral Services: Readings in Research*, ed. Larry VandeCreek, 23-32. Decatur, GA: Journal of Pastoral Care Publications, 1995. Originally published in *Bulletin of the American Protestant Hospital Association* (1973): 29-36.

________. "Effective Pastoral Care in the Hospital. In *At the Point of Human Need*, eds. J. Ashbrook, and J. Hinkle, Jr., 263-9. New York: University Press of America.

________. "Empirical Research in Pastoral Care and Counseling." In *Dictionary of Pastoral Care and Counseling*, ed. Rodney J. Hunter, 354-6. Nashville: Abingdon Press, 1990.

Flynn Smithe, Florence. "General Health Care Ministry." In *Health Care Ministry: A Handbook for Chaplains*, eds. Helen Hayes and Cornelius van der Poel, 114-32. New York: Paulist Press, 1990.

Foskett, John, and David Lyall. *Helping the Helpers: Supervision and Pastoral Care*. London: SPCK, 1988.

Fowler, J. W. "Faith/Belief." In *Dictionary of Pastoral Care and Counseling*, ed. Rodney J. Hunter, 394-97. Nashville: Abingdon Press, 1990.

________. *Stages of Faith: The Psychology of Human Development and the Quest for Meaning*. San Francisco: Harper and Row, 1981.

Frankl, Victor. *Man's Search For Meaning: An Introduction to Logotherapy*, 5th ed. London: Hodder and Stoughton, 1992.

Frend, W.H.C., "Pastoral Care; History - The Early Church." In *A Dictionary of Pastoral Care*, ed. Alastair V. Campbell, 190-2. London: SPCK, 1987.

Gaiser, Frederick J., ed. "Ministry and Mental Health." *Word and World* 9 (spring 1989): 109-73.

Gartner, John, John S. Lyons, David B. Larson, John Serkland, and Mark Peyrot. "Supplier-Induced Demand for Pastoral Care Services in the General Hospital: A Natural Experiment." In *Spiritual Needs and Pastoral Services: Readings in Research*, ed. Larry VandeCreek, 335-42. Decatur, GA: Journal of Pastoral Care Publications, 1995. Originally published in *The Journal of Pastoral Care* 44 no. 3 (1990): 262-70.

Gartner, John, David B. Larson, and Carole D. Vacher-Mayberry. "A Review of the Quantity and Quality of Empirical Research Published in Four Pastoral Counseling Journals: 1974-1985." *The Journal of Pastoral Care* 44, no. 2 (1990): 115-29.

Gerkin, Charles. *Crisis Experience in Modern Life*. Nashville: Abingdon Press, 1979.

Gibbons, James L., John Thomas, Larry VandeCreek, and Arne K. Jessen. "The Value of Hospital Chaplains: Patient Perspectives." *The Journal of Pastoral Care* 45 no. 2 (1991): 117-25.

Gibbs, H. W., and J. Achterberg-Lawlis. "Spiritual Values and Death Anxiety: Implications for Counseling with Terminal Cancer Patients." *Journal of Counseling Psychology* 25 (1978): 563-9.

Glueck, N. "Religion and Health: A Theological Reflection." *Journal of Religion and Health* 27 (1988): 109-18.

Gotjen, Arthur J. "Pastoral Dimensions of Health Care." Diss., Wesley Theological Seminary, n. d.

Goldberg, Alvin M. *Quality Circle in Health Care Facilities: A Model for Excellence*. Rockville, MD: Aspen Publishers, 1984.

Goldberg, Alvin M., and Carl C. Pegels. "The Quality Circle Process." In Quality Circles in Healthcare Facilities: A Model for Excellence. Rockville, Maryland: Aspen Publications, 1984.

________. "Basic Techniques of Quality Circles." In *Quality Circles in Healthcare Facilities: A Model for Excellence*. Rockville, Maryland: Aspen Publications 1984.

________. "Evaluation of Functioning Quality Circles." In *Quality Circles in Healthcare Facilities: A Model for Excellence*. Rockville, Maryland: Aspen Publications, 1984.

Graham, Nancy O. "Historical Perspective and Regulations Regarding Quality Assessment." In *Quality Assurance in Hospitals, Strategies of Assessment and Implementation*, 3-14. Rockville, Maryland: Aspen Publications, 1982.

Granstrom, S. L. "Spiritual Care for Oncology Patients." *Topics in Clinical Nursing* 7 (1985): 39-45.

Gravelle, John. "Clinical Theology." In *A Dictionary of Pastoral Care*, ed. Alastair V. Campbell, 38. London: SPCK, 1987.

Grigsby, Robert, J. Luther Mauney, and Myron Ebersole. "Creating Benchmarks for Pastoral Care: Issues for Department Managers." *The CareGiver Journal* 9 no.1 (1992): 11-13.

Gross, Joe. "A Model for Theological Reflection in Clinical Pastoral Education." *The Journal of Pastoral Care* 48 no. 2 (1994): 131-134.

Grossoehme, Danile H. "Closed-circuit TV and Videos in Pediatric Chaplaincy: Survey Results." *The CareGiver Journal* 12 no. 3 (1996): 28-31.

Guckenberger, Dale. "Developing a Volunteer Pastoral Care program." *In Chaplaincy Services in Contemporary Healthcare*, ed. Laurel Arthur Burton, 51-57. Schaumburg, Ill.: The College of Chaplains, 1992.

Gynther, Malcolm, and Kempson, Obert. "Attitudes Of Mental Patients and Staff Towards A Chaplaincy Program." *The Journal of Pastoral Care* 14, no. 4 (1960): 211- 17.

Haag, John E., and Linda H. Jackson "The Acceptance of Chaplains in Mental Hospitals." *American Benedictine Review*, 32, D (1981): 328-35.

Hall, Charles E. *Head and Heart: The Story of the Clinical Pastoral Education Movement*. Decatur, GA: Journal of Pastoral Care Publications, 1992.

Hackett, Earl. "Quality Assurance: An Asset for Chaplains." *The CareGiver Journal* 6 (1989): 128-41.

Haggard, Patricia. "Healing and Health Care of the Whole Person." *Journal of Religion and Health* 22, no. 3 (1983): 234-40.

Hahn, Jack A. L. "Fostering Human Values In Health Care Delivery." In *Clinical Pastoral Education and Health Care Delivery: Fifth Annual Conference of The Association for Clinical Pastoral Education 1972*, 13-20. Association of Clinical Pastoral Education, 1972.

Hall, C.M. "Crisis as Opportunity for Spiritual Growth." *Journal of Religion and Health* 25 (1986): 8-17.

Hall, Todd W, and Keith J. Edwards. "The Initial Development and Factor Analysis of the Spiritual Assessment Inventory." *Journal of Psychology and Theology* 24 no. 3 (1996): 233-46.

Halton, Mark R. "Faith and Medicine." *Christian Ministry* 24, no. 2 (1993): 7-20.

Hanley, Ann. "And the Prayer of Faith Will Save the Sick; Hospital Chaplaincy in Ireland." Confidential Survey of Hospital Chaplains regarding training and experiences of hospital chaplaincy. Maynooth, Ireland." Council for Research & Development, 1996. Typewritten.

________. "Major Religious Confidence Survey." *Intercom*, March 1998, 18-9.

Hanson, Karen R. "Minister as Midwife." *Journal of Pastoral Care* 50 no. 3 (1996): 249-56.

Hartung, B.M. "Pastoral Psychotherapy." In *Dictionary of Pastoral Care and Counseling*, ed. Rodney J. Hunter, 860-1. Nashville: Abingdon Press, 1990.

Hefferin, E. "Health Goal Setting: Patient-Nurse Collaboration at VA Facilities." *Milit Med* 144, 1979.

Helwig, Monika Konrad. "Pastoral Effectiveness." *Commonweal* 108, (January 30, 1981). 41-42.

Henning, Lawrence. "The Cross and Pastoral Care." *Currents in Theology and Mission* 13, no. 1 (1986): 22-29.

Herr, Vincent, William J. Devlin, and Frank J Kobler. *Religion and Mental Health: A Catholic Viewpoint*. New York: Academy of Religion and Mental Health, 1960.

Herth, K.A. "The Relationship Between Level of Hope and Level of Coping Response and Other Variables in Patients with Cancer." *Oncology Nursing Forum* 16, no. (1989): 67-72.

Hiatt, J. F. "Spirituality, Medicine, and Healing." *Southern Medical Journal* 79 (1986): 736-43.

Highfield, M.F., and C. Carson. "Spiritual Needs of Patients: Are They Recognized?" *Cancer Nursing* 6 (1983): 187-92.

Hill, Samuel S. Jr. "Theological Foundations for Healing Ministry", In *Clinical Pastoral Education and Health Care Delivery, The Fifth Annual Conference, Association of Clinical Pastoral Education, 1972*, 1-6. Association of Clinical Pastoral Education, 1972.

Holifield, E.B. "Pastoral Care Movement." In *Dictionary of Pastoral Care and Counseling*, ed. Rodney J. Hunter, 845-9. Nashville: Abingdon Press, 1990.

Holinger, Paul C. *Pastoral Care of Severe Emotional Disorders: Principles of Diagnosis and Treatment*. New York: Irvington Publications, 1985.

Holst, Lawrence E. *Hospital Ministry: The Role of the Chaplain Today*. New York: Crossroad, 1985.

________. "Initiating Pastoral Relationships." C*are Cassettes*, 6, no. 1 (1979) Chicago, Ill.: The College of Chaplains, 1979. Cassette, Side 1.

Houston, C. S., and W. E. Pasanen, "Patient Perceptions of Hospital Care." *Hospital Progress* 46 (1972): 70-4.

Hover, Margot, James L. Travis, III, Harold G. Koenig, and Lucille B. Bearson. "Pastoral Research in a Hospital Setting: A Case Study." *The Journal of Pastoral Care* 46 no. 3 (1992): 283-290.

Hoover, E.A. "Pastoral Psychology." In *Dictionary of Pastoral Care and Counseling*, ed. Rodney J. Hunter, 859-60. Nashville: Abingdon Press, 1990.

Hulme, William E. "New Life Through Caring Relationships in the Church." *Word and World* 2, no. 4 (1982): 340-52.

________. *Pastoral Care Comes of Age*. Nashville: Abingdon Press, 1970.

Hultgran, Arland J. ed. "Healing." *Word and World* 2 (fall 1982): 315-91.

Humphrey, Loren J. "New Insights on the Emotional Response of Cancer Patients and their Spouses: Where do they find help?" *The Journal of Pastoral Care* 49 no. 2 (1995): 149-56.

Hunter, R.J. "Moral Theology and Pastoral Care." In *Dictionary of Pastoral Care and Counseling*, 756-8. Nashville: Abingdon Press, 1990.

________. "Pastoral Care and Counseling (Comparative Terminology)." In *Dictionary of Pastoral Care and Counseling*, 845. Nashville: Abingdon Press, 1990.

Hurding, Roger. *Coping With Illness*. London: Hodder and Stoughton, 1988.

"Images of Wholeness: Interview with Laurence E. Sullivan." *Parabola* 18 (spring 1993): 4-13.

Jackson, E. N. "Calling & Visitation, Pastoral." In *Dictionary of Pastoral Care And Counseling*, ed. Rodney J. Hunter, 115-116. Nashville: Abingdon Press, 1990.

Jacobs, Charles M., Tom H. Christoffel, and Nancy Dixon. "Patient Care Audit." In *Measuring the Quality of Patient Care: The Rationale for Outcome Audit*, 1-10. Cambridge, MA: Ballinger Publishing Company, 1976.

Jennings, T.W., Jr. "Pastoral Theological Methodology." In *Dictionary of Pastoral Care and Counseling*, ed. Rodney J. Hunter, 862-4. Nashville: Abingdon Press, 1990.

Jergorian, Armen, D. "Theological Foundations for Healing Ministry." *Clinical Pastoral Education and Health Care Delivery, The Fifth Annual Conference, Association of Clinical Pastoral Education, 1972*, 11-12. Association of Clinical Pastoral Education, 1972.

Jimenez, Manuel J. "The Spiritual Healing of Post-Traumatic Stress Disorder at Menlo Park Veteran's Hospital." *Studies In Formative Spirituality* 14, no. 2 (1993): 175-87.

Johnson, Paul E. "A Theology of Pastoral Care." *Journal of Religion and Health* 3, no. 2 (1964): 171-5.

Johnson, Sarah C., and Bernard Spilka. "Coping with Breast Cancer: The Roles of Clergy and Faith." In *Spiritual Needs and Pastoral Services: Readings in Research*, ed. Larry VandeCreek, 183-98. Decatur, GA: Journal of Pastoral Care Publications, 1995. Originally published in *Journal of Religion and Health* 30 no. 1 (1991): 21-33.

Joint Commission on Accreditation of Hospitals. *An Introduction to Quality Improvement in Health Care: The Transition from QA to CQI.* Oakbrook Terrace, Ill: Joint Commission on Accreditation of Hospitals, 1991.

Jonsen, Albert R. "Ethical Decisions in Clinical Medicine." *The CareGiver Journal* 6 (1989): 1-6.

Justice, William G. *Don't Sit On The Bed: A Handbook for Visiting the Sick.* Nashville, Tennessee: Broadman Press, 1973.

Kahoe, R. D. *The Power of Religious Hope*. Paper presented at the annual meeting of the American Psychological Association, Washington, D.C., 1982.

Kaplan, Karen Orloff, and Julie M. Hopkins. *The QA Guide: A Resource for Hospital Quality Assurance*. Chicago: Joint Commission on Accreditation of Hospitals, 1980.

Kass, Jared. "Contributions of Religious Experience to Psychological and Physical Well-Being: Research Evidence and an Explanatory Model." In *Spiritual Needs and Pastoral Services: Readings in Research*, ed. Larry VandeCreek, 199-214, Decatur, GA: Journal of Pastoral Care Publications, 1995. Originally published in *The CareGiver Journal* 8 no. 4 (1991): 4-11.

Kearney Michael. *Mortally Wounded: Stories of Soul Pain, Death and Healing*. Dublin: Marino Press, 1996.

Kelly, David Francis, "Roman Catholic Medical Ethics and The Ethos of Modern Medicine." *Ephemerides Theologicae Lovanienses* 59, no. 1 (1983): 46-7.

Kenneally, Christy. *Communicating with the Sick and the Dying*. Dublin: Christy Kenneally Communications, 1982. Cassette.

Kinast, Robert A. "Caring for God's Covenant of Freedom: a Theology of Pastoral Care." In *Health Care Ministry: A Handbook for Chaplains*, eds. Helen Hayes and Cornelius Van der Poel, 7-21. New Jersey: Paulist Press, 1990.

________. "Pastoral Theology, Roman Catholic." In *Dictionary of Pastoral Care and Counseling*, ed. Rodney J. Hunter, 873-4. Nashville, Abingdon Press, 1990.

King, Dana E., and Bruce Bushwick. "Beliefs and Attitudes of Hospital Inpatients about Faith Healing and Prayer." *Journal of Family Practice* 39 no. 4 (1994): 349-52.

Klass, D., and A. Gordon. "Varieties of Transcending Experience at Death: A Videotape-based Study." *Omega* 9 (1978-9): 19-36.

Kline, C. B. "Providence, Doctrine of, and Pastoral Care." In *Dictionary of Pastoral Care and Counseling*, ed. Rodney J. Hunter, Nashville: Abingdon Press, 1990.

Kleinman, Arthur. *The Illness Narratives*. New York: Basic Books, 1988.

Knights, Ward, and Kramer, David. "Chaplaincy Role-Functions As Seen By Mental Patients And Staff." *The Journal of Pastoral Care* 18, no. 3 (1964): 154-60.

Koenig, Harold G. "The Relationship Between Judeo-Christian Religion and Mental Health Among Middle Aged and Older Adults." *Advances* 9, no. 4 (1993): 33-9.

________. "Religion and Mental Health in Later Life." In *Religion and Mental Health*, ed. John F. Schumaker, 177-88. New York: Oxford University Press, 1992.

Koenig, Harold G, Lucille B. Bearon, Margot Hover, and James L. Travis, III. "Religious Perspectives of Doctors, Nurses, Patients and Families." In *Spiritual Needs and Pastoral Services, Readings in Research*, ed. Larry VandeCreek, 153-70. Decatur, GA: Journal of Pastoral Care Publications, 1995. Originally published in *The Journal of Pastoral Care* 45 no. 3 (1991): 254-67.

Koenig, H., L. Bearon, and R. Dayringer. "Physician Perspectives on the Role of Religion in the Physician-Older Patient Relationship." *Journal of Family Practice* 28 (1988): 441-8.

Koenig, H., Kvale, J., and C. Ferrel. "Religion and Well-Being in Later Life." *Gerontologist* 28 (1988): 18-28.

Koenig, H., L. George, and J. Siegler. "The Use of Religion and Other Emotion-Regulating Coping Strategies Among Older Adults." *Gerontologist*, 28 (1988): 303-10.

Koenig, Harold G, Harvey J. Cohen, Dan G. Blazer, Carl Pieper, Keith G. Meador, FrankShelp, Veerainder Goli, and Bob DiPasquale. "Religious Coping with Depression among Elderly Hospitalized Medically Ill Men." In *Spiritual Needs and Pastoral Services: Readings in Research*, ed. Larry VandeCreek, 255-76, Decatur, GA: Journal of Pastoral Care Publications, 1995. Originally published in *American Journal of Psychiatry* 149 no. 12 (1992): 1693-1700.

Kriso, Kevin. "A Roman Catholic Perspective on Pastoral Care and Counseling." D. Min. term paper, Boston University, 1996.

Kroll, J., and W. Sheehan. "Religious Beliefs and Practices Among 52 Psychiatric Patients in Minnesota." *American Journal of Psychiatry* 146 (1989): 67-72.

Kuhn, C. "A Spiritual Inventory of the Medically Ill Patient." *Psychiatric Medicine* 6, (1988): 87-100.

Kunzman, Richard T. "An Assessment of the Ministry of Chaplains by Patients & Staff at the New England Rehabilitation Hospital, Woburn, MA." D. Min. diss, Boston University, 1984.

Landis, Homer Warren. "A Descriptive Evaluative Study of Ministry in Riverside Hospital Hospice, Newport News, Virginia." D. Min. diss. Boston University, 1983.

LaPierre, Larry, "A Chaplain's Group in a Short-Term Psychiatric Unit." *The CareGiver Journal* 12 no. 3 (1996): 22-7.

Lapsley, J.N. "Moral Dilemmas in Pastoral Perspectives." In *Dictionary of Pastoral Care and Counseling*, ed. Rodney J. Hunter, 752-55. Nashville: Abingdon Press, 1990.

Larson, D., E. Pattison, D. Blazer, A. Omran, and B. Kaplan. "Systematic Analysis of Research on Religious Variables in Four Major Psychiatric Journals, 1978-1982." *American Journal of Psychiatry* 143 (1986): 329-34.

Lawyer, John M. *Communication Skills For Ministry*. Dubuque, Iowa: Kendall Hunter Publishing Co., 1985.

LeFevre, Perry D., ed. "Spirituality and Pastoral Care." *Chicago Theological Seminary Register* 72, no. 3, (1982), 1-43.

Lewis, Douglass. "Do Psychology And Theology Speak The Same Language: A Comment on Mowrer's *The Crisis in Psychiatry and Religion*." *The Journal of Pastoral Care* 18, no. 3 (1964): 161-5.

Lipscomb, Harry. "Fostering Human Values In Health Care Delivery." *Clinical Pastoral Education and Health Care Delivery, The Fifth Annual Conference, Association of Clinical Pastoral Education, 1972*, 26-30. Association of Clinical Pastoral Education, 1972. 26-30.

Lindberg, Carter. "The Lutheran Tradition." In *Caring and Curing: Health and Medicine in the Western Religious Traditions*, 173-99. New York: McMillan Publishing Co. 1986.

Lloyd, Margaret. "Philosophy and Religion in the Face of Death and Bereavement " *Journal of Religion and Health* 35 no. 4 (1996): 295-310.

Loder, J. "Theology and Psychology." In *Dictionary of Pastoral Care and Counseling*, ed. Rodney J. Hunter, 1267-70. Nashville: Abingdon Press, 1990.

Lombard, Dalton. "Perceived need for, value of and role expectations of chaplains in hospital and community: results and implications of a survey in Malden, MA." D. Min. diss. Boston University, 1989.

Luke, Roice D., and Robert E. Modrow. "Professionalism, Accountability and Peer Review." In *Organization and Change in Healthcare Quality Assurance*, 3-11. Edited by Roice D. Luke, Janelle Krueger, and Robert Modrow. Rockville, Maryland, Aspen Publications, 1983.

Luke, Roice D., and Wayne R. Boss. "Barriers Limiting the Implementation of QualityAssurance Programs." In *Organization and Change in Healthcare Quality Assurance*, 147-155. Edited by Roice D. Luke, Janelle Krueger, and Robert Modrow. Rockville, Maryland: Aspen Publications, 1983.

Lyall, David. "Clinical Pastoral Education." In *A Dictionary of Pastoral Care,* ed. Alastair V. Campbell, 36-7.London: SPCK, 1987.

Madden, M.C. "Intimacy and Distance." In *Dictionary of Pastoral Care and Counseling*, ed. Rodney J. Hunter, 594-5. Nashville: Abingdon Press, 1990.

Maestri, William F. "Medicine and Religion: Battle Ground or Common Ground." *Linacre Quarterly* 52, no 3 (1985), 247-53.

Maddocks, Morris. "Spiritual Healing." In *A Dictionary of Pastoral Care*, ed. Alastair V. Campbell, 266-7. London: SPCK, 1987.

Magee, Brian. *Pastoral Care of the Sick.* Produced by Veritas Video Productions. 45 min. Dublin, 1984. Videocassette.

Mahoney, John. *Bioethics and Belief: Religion and Medicine in Dialogue.* London: Sheed and Ward, 1984.

Malherbe, A.J. "New Testament, Traditions & Theology of Care." In *Dictionary of Pastoral Care and Counseling*, ed. Rodney J. Hunter, 787-92. Nashville: Abingdon Press, 1990.

Malony, H. Newton. "Ministerial Effectiveness: A Review of Recent Research." *Pastoral Psychology* 33, (winter 1984), 96-104.

Markavich, Claudia, and Robert Voglewede. "Learning the Ten Step QA Process for Use in Pastoral Care Department: Part 1." *Journal of Quality Assurance* (March/April 1991): 10-5.

________. "Learning the Ten Step QA Process for Use in Pastoral Care Department: Part II." *Journal of Quality Assurance* (May/June 1991): 14-20.

Martin, C., C. Burrows, and J. Pomilio. "Spiritual Needs of Patients Study." In *Spiritual Care: The Nurse's Role*, eds. S. Fish, and J. Shelly, 160-76. Downer's Grove, Ill: Inter-Varsity Press, 1983.

Marty, Martin E. "Religion and Healing: The Four Expectations." *Second Opinion: Health, Faith and Ethics* 7 (1988), 61-80.

________. "The Tradition of the Church in Health and Healing." *International Review of Mission* 83, (April 1994), 227-245.

Marty, Martin E., and Kenneth Vaux, eds. *Health, Medicine and The Faith Tradition: An inquiry into religion and medicine.* Philadelphia: Fortress Press, 1982.

Mason, Randall C., Jr., Graham Clark, Robert B. Reeves, J., and S. Bruce Wagner. "Acceptance and Healing." In *Spiritual Needs and Pastoral Services: Readings in Research*, ed. Larry VandeCreek, 1-22. Decatur, GA: Journal of Pastoral Care Publications, 1992.

Originally published in *Journal of Religion and Health* 8 (1969): 123-42.

Massey, Elizabeth T. "Affirming Spirituality and Healing in Medicine." *The Journal of Pastoral Care* 50, no. 3 (1996): 235-7.

McAlister, W. Robert, and Charles W. Gusmer. "The Ministry of Healing in the Church: Roman Catholic–Pentecostal Dialogue. Rome. 1979." *One in Christ* 21 no.1 (1985): 43-60.

McCarthy, Jeremiah, and Judith Caron. *Medical Ethics: A Catholic Guide to Healthcare Decisions*, n. p. Liguori, 1990.

McCurdy, David. "Christ and Customers in Health Care and the Church." *The CareGiver Journal* 12 no. 3 (1996): 2-8.

McDonald, J.I.H. "The New Testament and Pastoral Care." In *A Dictionary of Pastoral Care*, ed. Alastair J. Campbell, 172-4. London: SPCK, 1987.

McCormick, Richard A. *The Critical Calling: Reflections on Moral Dilemmas Since Vatican II*. Washington DC: Georgetown University Press, 1989.

________. *Health and Medicine in the Catholic Tradition: Tradition in Transition.* New York: Crossword, 1987.

McGee, R. F., "Hope: A Factor Influencing Crisis Resolution." *Advances in Nursing Science* 6, no. 4 (1984): 34-44.

McGregor, T.S. "Hospital Chaplaincy." In *A Dictionary of Pastoral Care*, ed. Alastair V. Campbell, 117-8. London: SPCK, 1987.

McKenna, John T. "Religion and Medicine." *The Bulletin of the National Guild of Catholic Psychiatrists* 28 (1982): 66-78.

McSherry, E. "The Need and Appropriateness of Measurement and Research in Chaplaincy: Its Criticalness for Patient Care and Chaplain Department Survival post 1987." *Journal of Healthcare Chaplaincy* 1 no. 1 (1987): n. p.

McSherry, E., D. Kratz, and W. Nelson. "Pastoral Care Departments: More Necessary in the DRG Era?" H*ealth Care Management Review* 11, (1986): 47.

McSherry, Elisabeth, Megan Ciulla, and Laurel Arthur Burton. "Continuous Quality Improvement for Chaplaincy." In *Chaplaincy Services in Contemporary Healthcare*, ed. Laurel Arthur Burton, 33-42. Schaumburg, Ill: The College of Chaplains, 1992.

McSherry, Elisabeth, and Megan Ciulla. "The New Dynamic in Chaplain Management." *The CareGiver Journal* 8 no.1 (1991): 5-21.

McSherry, Elisabeth, and William A. Nelson. "The DRG Era: A Major Opportunity for Increased Pastoral Care Impact or a Crisis for Survival?" In *Spiritual Needs and Pastoral Services, Readings in Research*, ed. Larry VandeCreek, 309-24. Decatur, GA: Journal of Pastoral Care Publications, 1995. Originally published in *The Journal of Pastoral Care* 41 no. 3 (1987): 201-11.

Mickley, Jacqueline R., Karen Soeken, and Anne Belcher. "Spiritual Well-Being, Religiousness and Hope among Women with Breast Cancer." In *Spiritual Needs and Pastoral Services: Readings in*

Research, ed. Larry VandeCreek, 215-30. Decatur, GA: Journal of Pastoral Care Publications, 1995. Originally published in *IMAGE: Journal of Nursing Scholarship* 24 no. 2 (1992): 267-72.

Millar, John P. "Supervision, Pastoral." In *A Dictionary of Pastoral Care*, ed. Alastair V. Campbell, 272-3. London: SPCK, 1987.

Miller, J. F. "Assessment of Loneliness and Spiritual Well-Being in Chronically Ill and Healthy Adults." *Journal of Professional Nursing* 1 (1985): 79-85.

Miller, W. "Hospital Chaplaincy: 1984." *The Journal of Pastoral Care* 38, no. 2 (1984): 171-98.

Milles, L.O. "Pastoral Care (History, Tradition and Definition)." In *Dictionary of Pastoral Care and Counseling*, 836-44. Nashville: Abingdon Press, 1990.

Mills, Mitchell, Donald Mimbs, Edward E. Jayne, and Robert B. Reeves, Jr. "Prediction of Results in Open Heart Surgery." In *Spiritual Needs and Pastoral Services: Readings in Research*, ed. Larry VandeCreek, 33-9. Decatur: GA: Journal of Pastoral Care Publications, 1995. Originally published in *Journal of Religion and Health* 14 no. 3 (1975): 159-64.

Moberg, D. O. "Spiritual Well-Being of the Dying." In *Aging and The Human Condition*, ed. G. Lesnoff-Caravaglia, 139-55. New York: Human Sciences Press, 1982.

Montgomery, Carol L. "The Care-Giving Relationship: Paradoxical and Transcendental Aspects." *Alternative Therapies* 2 no. 2 (1996): 52-8.

Moltmann, Jurgen. *The Crucified God.* New York: Harper and Row, 1974.

________. "The Diaconal Church in the Context of the Kingdom of God." In *Hope for the Church*, n. p. Nashville: Abingdon Press, 1979.

Moore, Mary Kendrick. "The Role of Marketing and Public Relations in Pastoral Care." In *Chaplaincy Services in Contemporary Health Care*, ed. Laurel Arthur Burton, 70-80. Schaumburg, Illinois. The College of Chaplains, 1992.

Moore, Michael. "A Pastoral Care Narrative: Rosie's Stand." *The CareGiver Journal* 8 no.1 (1991) 39-41.

Mudd, E. R. "Spiritual Needs of Terminally Ill Patients" *Bulletin of American Protestant Hospital Association* 45 no. 3 (1981): 1-5.

Murray, Carolyn K. "Addressing your Patient's Spiritual Needs." *American Journal ofNursing* 95 no. 11 (1995): 159-61.

Myers, William R. *Research in Ministry: A Primer for the Doctor of Ministry Program.* Chicago: Exploration Press, 1993.

National Association for Pastoral Counseling and Psychotherapy. *Code of Ethics. Rules and Regulations* 1998. Dublin: National Association of Pastoral Counseling and Psychotherapy, 1998.

National Association of Catholic Chaplains, ed. *Pastoral Care of the Sick: A Practical Guide for the Catholic Chaplain in Health Care Facilities.* Washington, DC: United States Catholic Conference, 1974.

________. *To Heal As Jesus Did*, 3rd printing. New York: American Bible Society, 1976.

National Association of Hospital Chaplains. *Intensive Caring*. Produced by Kairos Communications. 50 min. Maynooth, Ireland, 1990. Videocassette.

Nelson, S. T., and Don S. Browning, eds. *Spirituality and Pastoral Care.* Philadelphia: Fortress Press, 1985.

Niklas, Gerald R. *The Making of a Pastoral Person*. New York: Alba House, 1996.

Niklas, Gerald, and Charlotte Stefanics. *Ministry to the Hospitalized.* New York: Paulist Press, 1975.

________. *Ministry to the Sick*. New York: Ala House, 1982.

"No Religious Right to Refuse Treatment Found." *Mental and Physical Disability Law Reporter* 8, no. 3 (1984): 283.

Nouwen, Henry. *Out of Solitude*. Notre-Dame, Indiana: Ave Maria Press, 1974.

________. *Creative Ministry*. New York: Doubleday & Co., 1979.

________. *The Living Reminder.* New York: Seabird Press, 1977.

________. *The Wounded Healer*. New York: Doubleday & Co., 1979.

Numbers, Ronald L., and David W. Amundsen, eds. *Caring and Curing: Health and Medicine in the Western Religious Traditions*. New York: MacMillan Publishing Company, 1986.

Oates, Wayne E. *The Bible in Pastoral Care*. Westminster: Westminster Press, 1953.

________. "Pastoral Care (Contemporary Methods, Perspectives and Issues)." In *Dictionary of Pastoral Care and Counseling*, 823-36. Nashville: Abingdon Press, 1990.

________. "Faith and Integrity, Pastors." In *Dictionary of Pastoral Care and Counseling*, ed. Rodney J. Hunter, 397-8. Nashville: Abingdon Press, 1990.

Oberst, Marilyn T. "Patient's Perceptions of Care: Measurement of Quality and Satisfaction." *Cancer* 53 no. 9 (1984): 2366-75.

O'Brien, M. E. "Religious Faith and Adjustment to Long–term Haemodialysis." *Journal of Religion and Health* 21, no. 1 (1982): 68-80.

O'Connell, Marvin R. "The Roman Catholic Tradition Since 1545." In *Caring and Curing: Health and Medicine in the Western Religious Traditions*, 108-145. New York: MacMillan Publishing Co., 1986.

O'Conner, A., C. Wicker, and B. Germino. "Understanding the Cancer Patient's Search for Meaning." *Cancer Nursing* 13 (1990): 167-75.

O'Donoghue, James A. "Collegiality: Essential Factor in Effective Health Care Ministry." *Hospital Progress* 63, no. 7 (1982): 21-3.

O'Rourke, Kevin, and Dennis Brodeur. *Medical Ethics: Common Ground for Understanding*. St. Louis, Missouri: Catholic Health Association of the United States, 1989.

Paloutzian, R. F., and C. W. Ellison. "Loneliness, Spiritual Well-Being and The Quality of Life." In *Loneliness: A Sourcebook of Current*

Theory, Research and Therapy, eds. L. A. Peplau, and D. Perlman, 224-36. New York: John Wiley & Sons, 1982.

Pangrazzi, Arnaldo. "Physicians & Clergy: Perspectives on Healing." *Linacre Quarterly* 50 (August 1983): 213-9.

Pargament, Kenneth I., David S. Ensing, Kathryn Falgout, Hannah Olsen, Barbara Reilly, Kimberley Van Haitsma, and Richard Warren. "God Help Me: (1): Religious Coping Efforts as Predictors of The Outcomes to Significant Negative Life Events." In *Spiritual Needs and Pastoral Services: Readings in Research*, ed. Larry VandeCreek, 79-117. Decatur, GA: Journal of Pastoral Care Publications, 1995. Originally published in *American Journal of Community Psychology* 18 no. 6 (1990): 793-824.

Park, C., L. H. Cohen, and L. Herb. "Intrinsic Religiousness and Religious Coping as Life Stress Moderators in Catholics versus Protestants." *Journal of Personality and Social Psychology* (1995).

Parkum, Kurt, H. "The Impact of Chaplaincy Services in Selected Hospitals in the Eastern United States." In *Spiritual Needs and Pastoral Services: Readings in Research*, ed. Larry VandeCreek, 325-33. Decatur, GA: Journal of Pastoral Care Publications, 1995. Originally published in *The Journal of Pastoral Care* 39 no.3 (1985), 62-9.

Patterson, George W. *The Cardiac Patient*. Minneapolis, MN: Augsburg Publishing House, 1978.

Patterson, Robert A. *Pastoral Health Care: Understanding The Church's Healing Ministries*. St. Louis, MO, 1983.

________. "Quality Assurance in Pastoral Care in Hospitals." *Pastoral Sciences* 5 (1986): 65-86.

Patton, M. Q. *How To Use Qualitative Methods in Evaluation*. Newbury Park, CA: Sage Publications, 1987.

________. *Qualitative Evaluation and Research Methods*. Newbury Park, CA: Sage Publications, 1991.

Penney, Dixianne. "Quality Assurance and the Mentally Ill: Perspectives from a Former Trustee." In *Quality Assurance in Hospitals: Strategies of Assessment and Implementation*, ed. Nancy O. Graham, 295-303. Rockville, Maryland: Aspen, 1982.

Peteet, J. "Religious Issues Presented by Cancer Patients Seen In Psychiatric Consultation." *Journal of Psychosocial Oncology* 3 (1985): 53-6.

Peterson, L. and A. Roy. "Religiosity, Anxiety, and Meaning and Purpose: Religion's Consequences for Psychological Well-Being." *Review of Religious Research* 27 (1985): 49-62.

Peterson, M. B. "Measuring Patient Satisfaction: Collecting Useful Data." *Journal of Nursing Quality Assurance 2* (May 1988): 25-35.

Peterson, Ralph E. "The Healing Church and Its Ministry." *Word and World* 2, no. 4 (1982): 322-9.

Philips, John L. Jr. *How To Think About Statistics*. 5th printing, New York: Freeman and Co. 1996.

Piacitelli, Henry J., and Joseph M. Wilcox. "Peer review and competence in ministry (proposals adopted by College of Chaplains)." *American Protestant Hospital Association Bulletin* 43, no. 2 (1979): 67-71.

Poel, Cornelius J. van der. "Evaluating Pastoral Care Activity." *Health Progress* 7 (September 1988): 79-81.

________. "Professionalism in Chaplaincy." In *Health Care Ministry: A Handbook for Chaplains*, eds. Helen Hayes and Cornelius van der Poel, 37- 49.New York: Paulist Press, 1990.

________. "Suffering and Healing: The Process of Growth." *Hospital Progress* 62 (fall 1981): 42-7.

Poling, James N., and Donald E. Miller. *Foundations For A Practical Theology of Ministry*. Nashville: Abingdon Press, 1985.

Pollner, M. "Divine Relations, Social Relations, and Well-Being." *Journal of Health and Social Behavior* 30 (1989): 92-104.

Pressman, Peter, John S. Lyons, David B. Larson, and James J. Strain. "Religious Belief, Depression and Ambulation Status in Elderly Women with Broken Hips." In *Spiritual Needs and Pastoral Services: Readings in Research*, ed. Larry VandeCreek, 119-24. Decatur, GA: Journal of Pastoral Care Publications, 1995. Originally published in *American Journal of Psychiatry* 147 no. 6 (1990): 758-60.

Princeton Religion Research Center. *Faith Development and Your Ministry*. Princeton, NJ: Princeton Religion Research Center. n.d.

Pruyser, P. *The Minister as Diagnostician*. Philadelphia, PA: Westminster Press, 1976.

Quinlan, John. *God Is With You: Hospital Notes and Prayers*, 2nd ed. Dublin: Veritas, 1995.

________. *Loved and Lost: The Journey Through Dying, Death and Bereavement*. Dublin: The Columbia Press, 1996 and Collegeville, MN: The Liturgical Press, 1997.

Radar, Blaine B. "Identification of Selected Personality Characteristics which make for Effectiveness in Pastoral Care." Ph.D. diss., Drew University, 1968.

Randolph, David James. *The Power That Heals: Love, Healing and the Trinity*. Nashville: Abingdon Press, 1994.

Reed, P. G. Death Perspectives and Temporal Variables in Terminally Ill and Healthy Adults." *Death Studies* 10 (1986): 443-54.

________. Religiousness in Terminally Ill and Healthy Adults. *Research in Nursing and Health*, 9 (1986): 35-41.

Reed, Pamela G. "Spirituality and Well-Being in Terminally Ill Hospitalized Adults." In *Spiritual Needs and Pastoral Services: Readings in Research*, ed. Larry VandeCreek, 51-66. Decatur, GA: Journal of Pastoral Care Publications, 1995. Originally published in *Research in Nursing and Health* 10 (1987): 335-44.

Reeves, Robert. "Healing and Salvation: A Clinical View." In *Healing and Religious Faith*, ed. Claude Frazier, 41-44. Philadelphia: United Church Press, 1974.

________. "The Use and Abuse of Religion in Sickness." *Care Cassettes*, 1, no. 1 (1974) Chicago, Ill.: The College of Chaplains. Cassette, Side 2.

________. *Healing and Salvation.* Chicago, Ill.: The College of Chaplains, 1974. Cassette, Side 2.

Renner, Jeri. "Ministry: A Paschal Process." *Camillian: Journal of The National Association of Catholic Chaplains*, n.d.: 3-7.

Rodgers, Carl R. *Client-Centered Therapy: Its content, practice, implications and theory*. London: Constable & Co., 1998 printing.

Rogers, Kenneth, H. "Preparation for Effective Pastoral Ministry." *Journal of Pastoral Care* 10, no.3 (1956), 161-169.

Rosen, Irving M. "Some Contributions of Religion to Mental & Physical Health." *Journal of Religion and Health* 13 (October 1974): 289-294.

Rossi, Ernest L. *The Psychobiology of Mind-Body Healing*. New York: W.W. Norton & Co., 1986.

Ruffing-Rahal, M. A. "The Spiritual Dimension and Well-Being Implications for the Elderly." *Home Healthcare Nurse* 2, no. 2 (1984): 12-3, 16.

Saudia, Theresa L, Marguerite R. Kenney, Kathleen C. Brown, and Leslie Young-Ward. "Health Locus of Control and Helpfulness of Prayer." In *Spiritual Needs and Pastoral Services: Readings in Research,* ed. Larry VandeCreek, 137-52. Decatur, GA: Journal of Pastoral Care Publications, 1995. Originally published in *Heart and Lung* 20 no. 1 (1991): 60-6.

Scarce Medical Resources and Justice. Braintree, MA: Pope John Center, 1987.

Schlauch, Chris R. "Expanding the Contexts of Pastoral Care." *The Journal of Pastoral Care* 44, no. 4 (1990): 359-371.

________. *Faithful Companioning: How Pastoral Counseling Heals.* Minneapolis: Fortress Press, 1995.

Schmidt, Franz. "Developing and Exploring A Pastoral Care Model in a Rural Hospital." D. Min. diss. Bethel Theological Seminary, 1992.

Schiller, P., and J. Levin. "Is There A Religious Factor in Health Care Utilization? A Review." *Social Science and Medicine* 27 (1988): 1369-79.

Schooler, Joseph C. "Fostering Human Values In Healthcare Delivery." *Clinical Pastoral Education and Health Care Delivery, The Fifth Annual Conference, Association of Clinical Pastoral Education*, 1972, 31-36. Association of Clinical Pastoral Education, 1972.

Schumaker, John F. ed. *Religion and Mental Health.* New York: Oxford University Press, 1992.

Seidl, Lawrence G. *Quality Assurance & Pastoral Care: Ally or Antagonist – Part 1.* 160 min. Decatur, GA: Journal of Pastoral Care Publications, 1992, Videocassette.

________. *Quality Assurance & Pastoral Care: Ally or Antagonist – Part II.* 60 min. Decatur, GA: Journal of Pastoral Care Publications, 1992, Videocassette.

Seybold, Klaus, and Ulrich B. Muller. *Sickness and Healing*. Translated by Douglas W. Scott. Nashville: Abingdon Press, 1981.

Shriver, Donald Woods Jr. *Medicine and Religion: Strategies for Care*. Pittsburgh: University of Pittsburgh, 1980.

Shupe, Anson, and Jeffrey K. Hades. "Understanding Unconventional Healing Models." *Second Opinion: Health, Faith and Ethics* 7 (1988), 82-103.

Simundsen, Daniel J. "Health and Healing in the Bible." *Word and World* 2, no. 4 (1982): 330-9.

Sivan Abigail B., George A. Fitchett and Laurel A. Burton. "Hospitalized Psychiatric and Medical Patients and the Clergy." *Journal of Religion and Health* 35 no. 1 (1996): 11-9.

Smith, Kermit, and Laurel Arthur Burton. "Chaplaincy at the Turn of the Century." In *Chaplaincy Services in Contemporary Healthcare,* ed. Laurel Arthur Burton, 104-6. Schaumburg, Ill: The College of Chaplains, 1972.

Snook, Lee E. "A Primer on the Trinity: Keeping Our Theology Christian." *Word and World* 2 no. 1 (1982): 5-16.

Soderstrom, K., and I. Martinson. "Patients' Spiritual Coping: A Study of Nurse and Patient Perspectives." *Oncology Nursing Forum* 14, (1987): 41-6.

Sofield, Loughlan, and Juliano Carroll. *Collaborative Ministry: Skills and Guidelines.* Notre Dame, Indiana 45665: Ave Maria Press, 1987.

Sofield, Loughlan, Juliano Carroll, and Rosine Hammett. *Design for Wholeness: Dealing with Anger/Learning to Forgive/Building Self-Esteem*. Notre Dame, Indiana 46446: Ave Maria Press, 1990.

Solean, John E. "Fostering Human Values In Health Care Delivery." *Clinical Pastoral Education and Health Care Delivery, The Fifth Annual Conference, Association of Clinical Pastoral Education,* 1972, 21-25. Association of Clinical Pastoral Education, 1972.

Sorcek, Paul M. "Developing A Healing Ministry of Prayer, Laying on of Hands, and Anointing of the Sick." D. Min. diss. Eastern Baptist Theological Seminary, 1986.

Spilka, B., and Spangler, J. *Spiritual Support in Cancer: Patient Encounters with Clergy.* Paper presented at the Convention of the Society for the Scientific Study of Religion, San Antonio, Texas.

Spilka, Bernard, John D. Spangler, and Constance B. Nelson. "Spiritual Support in Life Threatening Illness." In *Spiritual Needs and Pastoral Services: Readings in Research,* ed. Larry VandeCreek, 41-9. Decatur, GA: Journal of Pastoral Care Publications, 1995. Originally published in *Journal of Religion and Health* 22 no. 2 (1983): 98-104.

Spilka, B., J. Spangler, and M. Rea. "The Role of Theology in Pastoral Care of the Dying." *Theology Today* 38 (1981): 16-29.

Spilka, B., J. Spangler, M. Rea, and C. Nelson. "Religion and Death: The Clerical Perspective." *Journal of Religion and Health* 20 (1981): 299-306.

Spilka, B., L. Stout, B. Milton, and D. Sizemore. "Death and Personal Faith: A Psychometric Investigation." *Journal for the Scientific Study of Religion* 16 (1977): 169-78.

Stanley, William M. "Holistic Health Care for Person's Using A Rural Outpatient Clinic." D. Min. diss. Lancaster Theological Seminary, 1984.

Steere, David A., ed. *The Supervision of Pastoral Care*. Louisville, Kentucky: Westminster/John Knox Press, 1989.

Stoddard, Gregory, Earl A. Hackett, Roy Nash, and Jim Pierce. *Quality Assurance and Improvement: A Guide to Developing Continuous Quality Improvement Plans in Pastoral Care.* Schaumburg, Ill.: The College of Chaplains, 1992.

________. *Continuous Quality Improvement: An Update for 1994.* Schaumburg, Ill.: The College of Chaplains, 1994.

Stoll, R. "The Essence of Spirituality." In *Spiritual Dimensions of Nursing Practice*, V. B. Carson, 4-23. Philadelphia: W. B. Saunders, 1989.

________. "Spirituality: A New Perspective on Health." In *Paper Presented at the Conference on the Spiritual Dimension of Health at Marquette University College of Nursing*, Milwaukee, Wisconsin, 7 (1985): 1-7, 32.

Studdard, Al. Medical Ethics and The Church: interview by Watson E. Mills. 10 mins. *Catalyst Cassettes* 7, no. 7 (1975).

Stokes, Allison. *Ministry After Freud.* New York: Pilgrim Press, 1985.

Stone, Howard. "Word of God and Pastoral Care." *Encounter* 44, no. 4 (1983): 369-390.

________. "New Testament, Traditions and Theology of Care In." In *Dictionary of Pastoral Care and Counseling*, ed. Rodney J. Hunter, 787-92. Nashville: Abingdon Press, 1990.

Strasser, Stephen, and Rose Marie Davis. *Measuring Patient Satisfaction For Improved Patient Services*. Ann Arbor, Michigan: Health Administration Press, 1991.

Sullivan, Lawrence E. *Healing and Restoring: Health and Medicine in the World's Religious Traditions*. New York: MacMillan Publishing Company, 1989.

Sullivan, William M. "A New Ecology of Healing: Medicine and Religion in Holistic Care." *Listening* 19 (September 1984): 103-16.

Sydney, Australia, Council of Churches. *The Doctor and The Minister: A Discussion on Medical-Clerical Co-Operation for the Good of the Sick.* Sydney, Australia: Sydney Council of Churches, 1960.

Taggart, Sarah R. *Living As If: Belief Systems In Mental Health Practice*. San Francisco, CA: Jossey-Bass Inc., 1994.

Taylor, David M. "Clinical Pastoral Training." *The Journal of Pastoral Care* 16, no. 1 (1962): 34-40.

Taylor, Elizabeth Johnston and Madalon Amenta. "Cancer Nurses Perspectives on Spiritual Care: Implications for Pastoral Care." *The Journal of Pastoral Care* 48, no. 3 (1994): 259-65.

Taylor, Elizabeth Johnston. "Factors Associated with Meaning in Life among People with Recurrent Cancer." In *Spiritual Needs and Pastoral Services: Readings in Research,* ed. Larry VandeCreek, 291-308. Decatur, GA, Journal of Pastoral Care Publications 1995. Originally published in *Oncology Nursing Forum* 20 no. 9 (1993): 1399-1405.

Taylor, Marvin J. "Theological Foundations for Clinical Pastoral Education." *Clinical Pastoral Education and Health Care Delivery, The Fifth Annual Conference, Association of Clinical Pastoral Education, 1972*, 7-10. Association of Clinical Pastoral Education, 1972.

Thayer, Nelson S. T., and Browning Don S., eds. *Spirituality and Pastoral Care*. Philadelphia: Fortress Press, 1985.

Thomas, E. F. "People: Causes and Effects." In *Quality Circles In Healthcare Facilities: A Model for Excellence*, ed. Alvin M. Goldberg and Carl C. Pegels, 15-29. Rockville, Maryland: Aspen, 1984.

Thomas, J. M., Jr., and E. A. Weiner. "Psychological Differences Among Groups of Critically Ill Hospitalized Patients, and Well-Controls." *Journal of Consulting and Clinical Psychology* 42, (1974): 274-9.

Thomas, John. "Terminating Pastoral Relationships." *Care Cassettes,* 6 no. 7 (1979). Chicago, Ill.: The College of Chaplains. Cassette, Side 2.

Thomas John R, James Land, and Sigurd Sivertson. "Doctor-Clergy Relationships." *Care Cassettes*, Chicago, Ill.: The College of Chaplains, 1978. Cassette.

Thomas, Leo. *The Healing Team: A Practical Guide for Effective Ministry*. New York: Paulist Press, 1987.

Thornewill, Mark L "Quality Assurance Program for a Department of Pastoral Care." *American Protestant Hospital Association Bulletin* 46 no. 3 (1982) 144-8.

Thornton, Martin. "Pastoral Care: History-The Reformed Tradition." In *A Dictionary of Pastoral Care,* ed. Alastair V. Campbell, 192-3. London: SPCK, 1987.

Thornton, E. E., and H. N. Maloney. "Faith Healing." In *Dictionary of Pastoral Care and Counseling*, ed. Rodney J. Hunter, 401-406. Nashville: Abingdon Press, 1990.

Tillich, Paul. "The Theology of Pastoral Care." *Pastoral Psychology* 10, no.9 (1959): 22.

Tillman-Mowry, Leslie, and John Wilcher. "A Multidisciplinary Approach to the Care of the Heart Transplant Recipient with Emphasis on the Role of The Department of Pastoral Ministry." *The CareGiver Journal* 6 (1989): 22-35.

Tripp, Kevin F. "Certification of Health Care Personnel." In *Health Care Ministry: A Handbook for Chaplains,* eds. Helen Hayes and Cornelius van der Poel, 147-58. New York: Paulist Press, 1990.

Tucker, G. .M. "Old Testament & Apocrypha, Traditions & Theology of Care." In *Dictionary of Pastoral Care and Counseling,* ed. Rodney J. Hunter, 799-807. Nashville: Abingdon Press, 1990.

VandeCreek, Larry, ed. *Spiritual Needs and Pastoral Services: Readings in Research.* Decatur, GA: Journal of Pastoral Care Publications, 1995.

________. "Identifying the Spiritually Needy Patient: The Role of Demographics." In *Spiritual Needs and Pastoral Services: Readings in Research*, ed. Larry VandeCreek, 171-82. Decatur, GA: Journal of Pastoral Care Publications, 1995. Originally published in *The CareGiver Journal* 8 no. 3 (1991): 38-47.

________. "Pastoral Assessment of Selected Attitudes Among Hospital Patients and Family Members." *Sciences Pastorales* 11 (1992): 67-80.

________. "Research in the Pastoral Care Department." In *Chaplaincy Services in Contemporary Healthcare*, ed. Laurel Arthur Burton, 65-9. Schaumburg, Ill: College of Chaplains, 1972.

VandeCreek, Larry, Arne Jessen, John Thomas, James Gibbons, and Stephen Strasser. "Patient & Family Perceptions of Hospital Chaplains." In *Spiritual Needs and Pastoral Services: Readings in Research,* 343-56. Decatur, GA. Journal of Pastoral Care Publications, 1995. Originally published in *Hospital and Health Services Administration* 36 no. 3 (1991): 455-67.

VandeCreek, Larry, and Damain Smith. "Measuring the Spiritual Needs of Hospital Patients and Their Families." *The Journal of Pastoral Care* 46 no. 1 (1992), 46-52.

VandeCreek, Larry, Hilary Bender, and Merle Jordan. *Research in Pastoral Care and Counseling: Quantitative and Qualitative Approaches.* Decatur, GA: Journal of Pastoral Care Publications, 1994.

VandeCreek, Larry, and Loren Connell. "Evaluation of the Hospital Chaplains Pastoral Care: Catholic & Protestant Differences." *The Journal of Pastoral Care* 45 no. 3 (1991): 289-95.

VandeCreek, Larry, and Marjorie A. Lyon. "The General Hospital Chaplain's Ministry: Analysis of Productivity, Quality & Cost." *The CareGiver Journal* 9 no. 1 (1992): 3-10.

________. "Ministry of Hospital Chaplains: Patient Satisfaction." *Journal of Health Care Chaplaincy* 6 no. 2 (1997): 1-61.

________. "Preliminary Results From A Patient Satisfaction Instrument for Pastoral Care." *The CareGiver Journal* 9 no.1 (1992): 42-49.

VandeCreek, Larry, Marjorie A. Lyon, and John Devries. "Canadian Hospital Patients Evaluate their Chaplains Ministry." *Pastoral Sciences* 14 (1995), 133-45.

VandeCreek, Larry, and The Research Committees of the American Association of Pastoral Counseling and The Association of Clinical Pastoral Education. *A Research Primer for Pastoral Care and Counseling*. Decatur, GA: Journal of Pastoral Care Publications, 1988.

VandeCreek, Larry, Susan Benes, and Christina Nye. "Assessment of Pastoral Needs Among Medical Outpatients." In *Spiritual Needs and Pastoral Services: Readings in Research*, 277-90. Decatur, GA: Journal of Pastoral Care Publications, 1995. Originally published in *The Journal of Pastoral Care* 47 no. 1 (1993): 44-53.

Vastyan, E. A. "Spiritual Aspects of the Care of Cancer Patients." *Cancer Journal for Clinicians* 36 (1986): 110-4.

Vatican II. *The Documents of Vatican II: All Sixteen Official Texts Promulgated By The Ecumenical Council* 1963-1965. London: Geoffrey Chapman, 1966.

Wagner, D. M. "Quality Assurance: A Professional Responsibility." *Caring* 5 (January 1988): 46-49.

Watson, Jean. "Delivery and Assurance of Quality Health Care: A Rights Based Foundation." In *Organization and Change In Health Care Quality Assurance*, 13-9. Edited by Roice D. Luke, Janelle Krueger, and Robert Modrow. Rockville, Maryland: Aspen Publications, 1983.

Weidman-Gibbs, H., and J. Achterberg- Lawlis. "Spiritual Values and Death Anxiety: Implications for Counseling Terminal Cancer Patients." *Journal of Counseling Psychology* 25 (1978): 563-9.

Weikart, Robert Curtis. "Clinical Collaboration between Clergy and Physicians." D. Min. diss., United Theological Seminary, Dayton, 1982.

________. "When the Doctor and the Minister Disagree." *Hastings Center Report* 14 (1984): 30-1.

Welch, Amy. "Chaplaincy: A Religion & Medicine Partnership." *Chaplaincy Services in Contemporary Health Care*, ed. Laurel Arthur Burton, 9-14. Schaumburg, Illinois: The College of Chaplains, 9-14.

Wesley, Dick. *Redemptive Intimacy: A New Perspective for the Journey to Adult Faith.* Mystic, CT: Twenty-Third Publications, 1981.

Whitmer, Marlin. "Umbrella for Caring." *The CareGiver Journal* 6 (1989): 7-21.

Wilcox, Paul S. "The Church's Role in Whole Person Medicine: A Model for Teaching and Action." D. Min. diss. Boston University, 1983.

Wise, Carroll A. *The Meaning of Pastoral Care*. New York: Harper and Row, 1966.

Whyte, James A. "Pastoral Care: History-The Reformed Tradition." In *A Dictionary of Pastoral Care*, ed. Alastair V, Campbell, 193-5. London: SPCK, 1987.

________. "Practical Theology." In *A Dictionary of Pastoral Care*, ed. Alastair V. Campbell, 212-3. London: SPCK, 1987.

Willis, R. Wayne. "The Hard and Soft in Healthcare." *Journal of Religion and Health* 34 (summer 1995): 99-103.

Wilkinson, John. *Health and Healing: Studies in New Testament Principles and Practice*. Edinburgh: The Hansel Press, 1980.

________. "The Concept of Health in the Old Testament." In *Health and Healing: Studies in New Testament Principles and Practice*, 3-8. Edinburgh: The Handsel Press, 1980.

________. "The Words for Health in the New Testament." In *Health and Healing: Studies in New Testament Principles and Practice*, 9-12. Edinburgh: The Handsel Press, 1980.

________. "The Definition of Health in the New Testament." In *Health and Healing: Studies in New Testament Principles and Practice*, 13-8. Edinburgh: The Hansel Press, 1980, 13-18.

________. "The Records of Healing" (in the Gospels)." In *Health and Healing: Studies in New Testament Principles and Practice*, 19-34. Edinburgh: The Hansel Press, 1980.

________. "The Approach to Healing (in the Gospels)." In *Health and Healing: Studies in New Testament Principles and Practice*, 36-46. Edinburgh: The Handsel Press, 1980.

________. "The Methods of Healing (in the Gospels)." In *Health and Healing: Studies in New Testament Principles and Practice*, 47-60. Edinburgh: The Handsel Press, 1980.

Willey, Frank T. "The Chaplain as Mediator: A Ministry of Presence and Productivity." *The CareGiver Journal* 6 (1989): 77-89.

Woods, Neville B. *The Healings of the Bible*. New York: Hawthorn Books, 1958.

YaDeau, Richard E., MD, "Healing." *Word and World* 2, no. 4 (1982): 317-21.

Yates, J., B. Chamber, P. St. James, M. Follensbee, and F. McKegney. "Religion in Patients with Advanced Cancer." *Medical and Pediatric Oncology,* 9 (1981): 121-8.

Young-Manus, Maureen. "The Evaluation of Pastoral Care By Hospital Administrators: A Survey For Profit and Non-profit Making Institutions." Ph.d. diss. Boston University: 1989.

Subject Index

Note: Some entries that appear throughout the book such as Healing, Pastoral Relatedness, Pastoral Relationship, Patient Satisfaction and Research are not listed in the Subject Index

Index of Persons

John Quinlan, a priest of the Diocese of Kerry, Ireland, is Director of Pastoral Care/Counselling and of Clinical Pastoral Education (CPE) in Tralee General Hospital, Tralee, Co. Kerry, Ireland. He received his Doctor of Ministry degree from Boston University, and is certified as a CPE Supervisor by the Association of Clinical Pastoral Education, Ireland (ACPEI). Dr. Quinlan is an Accredited Member of the National Association for Pastoral Counseling and Psychotherapy (NAPCP) in Ireland. His previous publications include *God Is With You: Hospital Notes and Prayers* (Veritas Publications, Dublin, 2nd edition, 1995), and *Loved and Lost: the journey through dying, death, and bereavement* (The Columba Press, Dublin, 1996; and The Liturgical Press, Collegeville, Minnesota 56321, 1997).